GOD'S WORDS

Perfect, Reliable and True

GOD'S WORDS
Perfect, Reliable and True

BRET CARTER

GOSPEL
ADVOCATE
A TRUSTED NAME SINCE 1855

Published by Gospel Advocate Co.
1006 Elm Hill Pike, Nashville, TN 37210
www.gospeladvocate.com

ISBN 10: 0-89225-599-4
ISBN 13: 978-0-89225-599-3

DEDICATION

FOR DAD, UNCLE JACK AND UNCLE DAVE –

THE THREE PATRIARCHS

WHO TAUGHT ME TO LOVE THE TRUTH.

"WE HAVE BEEN DEFINING AND REFUTING: IT REMAINS FOR US TO OFFER OUR PROOFS; BUT WE APPEAL SOLELY TO THE WORD OF GOD, WHICH ALONE CAN FURNISH THEM. IF GOD REVEALS HIMSELF, IT IS FOR HIM TO TELL US, IN THAT REVELATION, IN WHAT MEASURE HE HAS VOUCHSAFED TO DO SO. FAR FROM US BE VAIN HYPOTHESIS! THEY WOULD CONTAIN NOUGHT BUT OUR OWN CONCEITS, TO DAZZLE THE EYE OF OUR FAITH. WHAT SAY THE SCRIPTURES? IS THE SOLE QUESTION."

LOUIS GAUSSEN (1790–1863)

THEOPNEUSTIA: THE PLENARY INSPIRATION OF THE HOLY SCRIPTURES (1841)

TABLE OF CONTENTS

Foreword

A CHALLENGE

Have you ever wondered about the inspiration, power and reliability of the Bible? Is it truly the Word of God? Is it really inspired? If so, what does that actually mean? In fact, just how "inspired" is it?

Through the centuries, and perhaps never more so than now, man has both had doubts and cast doubts on the reliability and inspiration of the Bible. Is it perfect or just pretty good reading? Is the Bible the absolute Word of God, infallible and trustworthy in every way to lead us to salvation? Or is it more like a guidebook, a signpost on the road of life that simply points in the general direction of redemption?

God's Words: Perfect, Reliable and True asks these very questions in a simple and straightforward way. It will challenge each us to evaluate just how we think of the Word of God and, hopefully, encourage each of us to reestablish the close, intimate and trustworthy relationship with the Bible that God intended.

Whether you are a new Christian or a veteran warrior, *God's Words* can strengthen your resolve both to trust and to spend time in God's Word. It can encourage and increase in all of us our devotion to seeking out the truths within its pages. If it in fact does these things, then it will have accomplished what the author intended. May God bless you as your devotion to His Word grows.

– Mike Byron
V.P. of Hyland Christian School board, Westminster, Colo.

Preface

FOR SKEPTICS AND BELIEVERS

W e have written pages and pages and pages about the Bible. Books about the Word of God fill thousands of shelves in libraries all over the world. Scripture itself points out that "the writing of many books is endless" (Ecclesiastes 12:12). When it comes to scribbling down our thoughts about the Bible, mankind has never found itself at a loss for words.

And now, here is another – one of the countless books somehow convinced it might have something more to say, even though the Bible also points out "there is nothing new under the sun" (Ecclesiastes 1:9). Yet when it comes to mankind's tendency to misunderstand the nature of the Word of God, here too we also discover nothing is new. We still struggle. For the most part, our perception of the Word is clouded and corrupted, hindering our search for the Truth. Once again, maybe there are reasons for yet another book to speak up on the issue.

Because of so many differing perspectives about the Bible, this book is intended for those who might consider themselves skeptics, but it is also meant to be of use to those who consider themselves believers. Even in this latter group, there are a variety of perceptions about the Word. Some think the Bible is just a helpful guide. Others consider it to be more than that. But even among these hopeful few, the extent of this is still hazy in their minds.

Many of us hesitate. There are discussions about contradictions in Scripture. There are arguments about the limitations of the Bible. There are books about the imperfections and flaws in the Word of God. So we pause, unsure of whether to welcome the Word with open arms.

Some of you are beginning to suspect the real possibility that the Bible is absolutely accurate, that it is completely trustworthy, and that it is perfectly true. Countless writers are eager to line up and express their thoughts on the matter. But this small book is intended only to point to Scripture. This book will hopefully find a way past its own pages – and past the pages of all other books *about* the Bible – to the pages of the Bible itself. For if the Bible is actually what it claims to be, then it is the only book that has ever truly mattered.

Chapter 1

ON THE SAME PAGE

T here was some confusion. The Bible class was in the middle of a discussion about Eutychus – the young man who fell out of the window during Paul's sermon, as mentioned in Acts 20. After the passage was read out loud, one of the students said, "I don't get it."

So they read the passage again.

The student still looked puzzled. "I don't get it."

Because the student was normally insightful, it was unexpected that he would have such a difficult time grasping this simple story in Scripture. It was pretty straightforward. A young man fell out of a window and died. Not complicated.

To help the student understand, the teacher resorted to paraphrasing. "Paul was preaching for a long time, and it was getting late. This guy Eutychus was sitting in the window listening, and he fell asleep. And then he fell out of the window. Three floors down is quite a drop. So the fall killed him."

A light bulb appeared over the student's head. "Oh!"

There had been a misunderstanding. The student had not realized Eutychus had died from falling. The student thought Paul's sermon itself had proven to be fatal to Eutychus. A reading of the New International

Version can be misunderstood: "Seated in a window was a young man named Eutychus, who was sinking into a deep sleep as Paul talked on and on. When he was sound asleep, he fell to the ground from the third story and was picked up dead" (Acts 20:9). The student genuinely thought Eutychus had died of boredom. Notice that Eutychus "fell to the ground from the third story and was picked up dead." From a certain angle, it does seem like Paul told one too many stories and poor Eutychus just couldn't take it anymore.

This might serve as an inadvertent cautionary tale for preachers who don't know when to quit. But maybe it can also serve as an example of our tendency to get confused.

It is very possible to talk about the same thing and yet not be talking about the same thing. This can be a source of much amusement. Unfortunately, it can also have darker consequences.

CONFUSION ABOUT THE BIBLE

On a much grander scale, there is confusion surrounding the Bible. It is just one book, yet people have reached a vast array of different conclusions concerning what it has to say. Thousands of different and contradictory beliefs can be traced back to this single book. The Bible stands at one end, and on the other end are a thousand beliefs, each claiming the Bible as its point of origin.

When it comes to the Bible, we often think we are talking about the same thing, but actually we are not.

Unfortunately, this one book seems to be different for each person who picks it up. It often becomes an extension of the reader, custom-tailored to support whatever ideas might have found their way into the reader's head. When that same reader encounters another reader of the Bible who has reached different conclusions, the Bible then becomes a platform upon which to build all kinds of animosity.

The Word of God has become a source of division. It is a book that fragments humanity into frowning pieces. Frustrated, we often turn our back on this conflict, using catchphrases such as "That's your interpretation." This seems to suggest that the Bible is a book subject to the whims of whoever lays eyes on it. It is reduced to nothing more than a glorified inkblot in which we see only what we want to see.

That's a problem.

There are those who suggest something is wrong with the book. Maybe its nature automatically eludes conclusions. Maybe it is unavoidably vague and offers no definite insight about truth. If it is inherently "fuzzy," then it is merely something to be used to a limited extent. Any efforts to derive something greater will result only in seeds of contention, nurturing the tension between opposing ideas.

Or maybe the book is not the problem. The problem might be in the people who pick up the book. The problem might be that not everyone agrees about the nature of the Bible. It could be like the student confused about Eutychus. We only *think* we are talking about the same thing.

INEVITABLE CONCLUSIONS

Our perspective of the Bible will shape the way we apply our minds to it. Our concept of its truth is already sketched out to a certain extent even before we open the book. If we think that the Bible is a collection of religious writings, we will reach certain conclusions. If we think that the Bible is a general guideline for living a good life, we will reach another set of conclusions. If we think that the Bible is truly the Word of God, we will reach yet another set of conclusions.

Just what exactly is this book? Until that question is answered, there is no moving forward. Or rather, there is no moving forward without veering off into a thousand separate directions.

Is this the Word of God, mostly the Word of God, or sort of the Word of God? When we open these pages, to what degree can we rely on the fact that it came from the Creator?

TWO KINDS OF EVIDENCE

We do not have to resort to guesswork. There is evidence to be weighed. In this particular case, there are two kinds of evidence – external and internal.

External evidence comes into play when the Bible is placed alongside the secular information collected over generations. All the findings of archaeology, biology, textual criticism, anthropology and biochemistry are presented as "outside" evidence concerning the reliability of the Bible. If the Bible were the defendant in a trial, these findings would be the "witnesses" brought in to testify about the integrity and character of the defendant.

A thorough and fair examination in this manner always reveals that the Bible can stand up even under close investigation. In times past, secular "truths" have opposed Scripture, claiming that the Word is inaccurate. Inevitably, the accusation is retracted as new information surfaces, and the Bible remains tried and true. This is external evidence.

There is also **internal evidence**. This would be the equivalent of letting the defendant testify on his own behalf. Concerning the Bible, some suggest this is a waste of time – letting a book vouch for its own reliability. But we would do no less for a defendant put on the stand. The character and integrity of a person can indeed be derived from what he has to say. Just as any contradiction or obvious duplicity might disqualify someone as trustworthy, an investigation that revealed the person to be completely consistent and honest would reveal the true nature of the person.

Examining the external evidence is certainly a worthwhile endeavor. Yet it must be pointed out that this involves judging the Bible by the testimony of sources that are themselves often inconsistent and flawed. In essence, external evidence is man critiquing God. What follows in this book is a presentation of the internal evidence.

FOUR BASIC TRUTHS

In order to build this analysis effectively, it is vital to establish four basic truths as a foundation.

(1) God exists. "His invisible attributes, His eternal power and divine nature, have been clearly seen" (Romans 1:20). Based on all the evidence, both secular as well as scriptural, this might seem to be a given. But it is vital to establish an anchor with this fact: there is a Creator who exists. And He doesn't just command some tangent, religious realm, but every facet of this existence. [1]

(2) God is involved. "For the eyes of the LORD move to and fro throughout the earth that He may strongly support those whose heart is completely His" (2 Chronicles 16:9). God is not a vague power that exists in the vicinity of earth. He is not just a "force" that has general good feelings toward the world. God is omnipresent and deeply active

---

1 Job 12:7-9; Psalm 19:1-6; Hebrews 11:6

in His creation. He allows for free will, but in the grand scheme of things, His own will rises triumphant. [2]

(3) God is omnipotent. Scripture says "with God, all things are possible" (Matthew 19:26). This means He is all-powerful. We are dealing with Someone who has unlimited capability. As God, He is able to accomplish whatever He wants. [3]

(4) God is omniscient. "Even the darkness is not dark to You, and the night is as bright as the day" (Psalm 139:12). God is all-knowing. He is not "in the dark" about anything. He is fully informed about everything that has ever occurred and everything that has yet to occur. [4]

These will be treated as basic assumptions. Any doubts surrounding these statements might be obstacles to continuing with this particular study.

THREE POSSIBILITIES

It is important to have something solid to stand on. We live in a time that seems convinced that reality is dependent upon our perception of it. Apparently, individuals can fashion their own version of "what's going on" as long as they are sincere about it. Whatever they wish, so it is.

Regardless of our imaginations, reality is an indestructible and strict landscape with real consequences. Our fond ideas will not survive forever. We may browse through life and construct some kind of "belief system," but reality moves for no man.

If there is a God, our sophisticated ponderings do not change this fact. If the Bible is the Word of God, our perspective of it does not alter that either.

With all this in mind, let's consider these potential views:

• The Bible is completely false and is only a collection of interesting fictional stories.

• The Bible is partially reliable and can best serve as a general guide.

• The Bible is the Word of God, written and compiled completely by the Creator, and can be trusted without reservation.

---

2 Psalm 139:7-10; Proverbs 15:3; Jeremiah 16:17; Zechariah 4:10; Ephesians 1:11; Colossians 1:17; Romans 8:28
3 Genesis 18:14; Job 42:2; Jeremiah 32:17
4 Psalm 50:11; Psalm 139:2; Isaiah 37:28

AVOIDING AGENDAS

What we choose to believe about the Bible will ultimately determine what we choose to believe. And this must be approached with some caution. Any conclusion is suspect because of our own human nature. Anyone who has ever taken a literature class knows it is possible to make a book say anything you want it to say. Armed with a highlighter and an overactive imagination, one can find meaning in everything and nothing. That "meaning" can then serve whatever purpose might be ruling the reader's mind at the time.

We are in the midst of an epic argument. There are those who feel compelled to attack the Bible. With brief lunges, they expose "contradictions" or "flaws." Anyone can do a fly-by and come away confident he has reduced the Bible to a fable.

Maybe closer to home, it is also very easy just to browse through Scripture and find support for conclusions we have made before the fact. Taking things "out of context" is always a potential danger. All of us are probably guilty of doing this at one time or another. It takes great effort to keep one's mind open and try not to finagle the Word to fit our ideas.

So when it comes to seeking the truth, it takes effort for us not to get in the way. It is important that we step cautiously and approach the Bible with eyes and minds wide open. Although the Bible might be solid truth, our approaches to it are often not so solid. Agendas lurk inside all of us. It is relatively easy to manipulate pieces of the Bible, taking scriptures out of context to serve our own will rather than God's.

The commotion surrounding the Bible has produced countless ideas. All kinds of people are lined up to tell you what to believe. The book you hold in your hand is just one of many. Whether this book or any other book has anything valid to say is certainly up for debate. But this book was written with the hope that even if we end up throwing away all the eager "insight" offered by anyone, ultimately we will allow the Bible itself to have some input on the matter.

QUESTIONS

1. What are some common influences that might shape someone's approach to the Bible?

2. If someone thinks of God's Word as a book of guidelines, how will this shape his relationship to it?

3. What specific parts of the Bible are typically the favorites of people in general? Why?

4. What are some of the less popular parts of the Bible? What are some possible explanations for that?

5. When it comes to Scripture, why is external evidence, to a certain extent, secondary in comparison to internal evidence?

6. How might believing in God's omnipotence be a crucial factor in one's conclusions about the Bible? His omniscience?

7. How do people often construct their own personal "belief system"?

8. What are some biblical passages that are often misquoted or misapplied?

9. If the Bible is only partially true, how might this affect one's conclusions about the Bible?

10. If the Bible is completely true, how might this affect one's conclusions about the Bible?

Chapter 2

SETTING SAIL

Sometimes you wonder if there's a conspiracy. Although it might be easy to imagine a league of intellectuals intentionally twisting words and phrases in order to promote confusion, this is not the case. Complications surface without design. It's just the way language works.

Time tampers with words. There are words that fall in and out of favor. There are words that fade into extinction, obsolete and forgotten. Definitions can shift. If enough years go by, words that once meant one thing can now mean another.

The word "artificial" originally meant "full of artistic skill." The word "awful" was first used to describe something amazing, causing you to be "full of awe." These two words have drastically changed. What was once artistic and amazing is now fake and horrible.

At some point, someone possibly misused a particular word and threw the meaning out of alignment. Then this was carried on by the next person to the next, ultimately resulting in a drastic transformation of meaning. Unintentionally, we corrupt our communication.

No doubt there have also been intentional efforts to warp words. Words are potent, and what we say controls the way we think. Those who are in charge have often spun definitions in directions to serve their own purposes.

Euphemisms abound in the news. When civilians are killed in a war, it's called "collateral damage." When someone lies, it's called "disinformation." This cushioning of the facts can contribute to misunderstandings. Regardless of the true culprit, words are powerful, and it often takes effort to derive durable concepts. It is important we find meaning beneath the babble.

Words are altered for a variety of reasons, but regardless of why, this semantic drift adds to the confusion of religion. There are some words, because of the world's disregard for them, that have been drained of any real meaning. Words such as "holy" and "atonement" are quarantined to obscurity. The average person has no idea what they mean. They are simply religious words that float in and out of hearing whenever there is a religious activity of some sort.

However, truth is often sabotaged when scripturally significant words become completely unraveled and refashioned into lesser concepts that fall short of their true meanings. For example, in contemporary conversation, the word "saint" is often used to mean a famous religious historical figure via Catholicism – usually associated with some fantastical act that is said to have verified them as a person of great spirituality and power. At the very least, the word "saint" is used to describe someone with strong religious convictions or an overly good person, as in "I'm no saint." (It's interesting we often use the word to identify what we are *not*.)

However, this modern use of "saint" does not match the original use. The Bible (the book from which the term "saint" originated) uses the word to mean a Christian (Ephesians 1:1). By true definition, every Christian is a saint.

The same is true of the word "priest." According to the Bible, all Christians are priests (1 Peter 2:9). Yet if you were to use this word in a conversation today as it was originally intended, it would result in confusion or even animosity. Time and ignorance have confused our terminology. [1]

---

1 The word "miracle" is another example. We use the term loosely. Phrases such as "the miracle of birth" are relatively misleading. A miraculous event was something out of the norm. It was a supernatural event that shook the everyday world. It was meant to be an attention-getter that proclaimed authority (Luke 5:24). As beautiful and amazing as the birth of a baby might be, it is not a miracle by its strictest definition. Birth happens all the time. It is important to understand that altering the basic definition of words can lessen the impact they were meant to have.

A KEY DEFINITION

There is no denying that our sloppy usage of words can cause them to lose their ability to affect us in the way they were originally intended to. The same is true with the word "inspiration." We have grown used to the idea that someone can be "inspired" by a sunset or "inspired" by a movie. Because of this loose application of the word, we might fail to fully grasp the significance of its use in the Bible. "All Scripture is inspired by God and profitable for teaching, for reproof, for correction, for training in righteousness" (2 Timothy 3:16). Tainted by the world's definition, we might imagine Moses or Paul merely drawing on their own human wisdom as they enjoyed a moment of quiet reflection. If "inspired" only means that someone was once emotionally or intellectually stirred up, then our idea of the Bible is already off to a bad start.

The word "inspired" in the original Greek is *theopneustos*. It literally means "God-breathed." This means something far more than what might be connected with a sunset or a movie. The Bible is making the claim that all things falling under the category of "Scripture" are to be considered "God-breathed." This is an essential, basic truth that must be in place before we make any headway concerning the nature of the Bible. "God-breathed" means more than "inspiration" on a human level – much more.

There is some discussion about how much of the Bible is inspired or what level of inspiration is involved. Some believe that God gave the gist of what He wanted to say, and then the writers elaborated. Others believe that He was more involved than that. There is even the concept of "plenary" (full, complete) inspiration, which suggests that every word contained in the Bible was directed by God. This is where many beliefs part ways.

If the inspiration of the Bible is somewhat hazy, this leaves much room for personal interpretation. [2]

If, on the other hand, the Bible is fully inspired by God on a deep level, there isn't any room for amendments or loopholes. It becomes

---

2 There is no escaping interpretation. But we often use this word in a distorted sense as well. In this day and age, people seem to think that their views are valid simply because they have them. Everybody's opinion is given a certain amount of admiration or consideration even if it is not based on anything that might be considered authority. People simply think something,

difficult to twist. Regardless of how offensive it might be to our modern sense of morals, it remains a solid rock – uncompromising and bold.

THE FORK IN THE ROAD

The Bible makes no apologies. The book makes some pretty extreme claims. "Your Word is truth" (John 17:17). "The law of the LORD is perfect" (Psalm 19:7). "The sum of Your word is truth" (119:160). These are not half-hearted statements. Nothing suggests that the reader should take things with a grain of salt. The Bible is the Truth, not something resembling the Truth. And if the Bible is indeed the perfect Truth, this means we are to take every part of it very seriously.

If "all Scripture is God-breathed," as recorded in 2 Timothy 3:16 (NIV84), then this is the fork in the road. If we approach the Bible as anything less than the words of God, we are on a different path. If we believe this book does not hold the words of God, then we set out on a path with a series of complicated twists and turns. We will then be confronted by several turning points where we must decide which parts are to be taken as truth and which parts are to be taken as something that is "truth-ish." If this is the case, we must regroup and offer adapted phrases along the lines of "Your Word is mostly truth" or "the law of the LORD is nearly perfect." Even at this early stage, we are already talking about two different books.

There is a big difference between a book that is the Word of God and a book that is the word of the godly. The first will not bend to the will of man. The second will serve as a tool for just about any idea man might fashion. The concept of partial inspiration opens the door to much confusion.

It is the in-between position that proves to be a great source of conflict. If the Bible is simply a collection of made-up fables, then we can call it a day and begin trying to build a shaky life based on an existence that came out of nowhere and is heading nowhere. If the

---

and it becomes good enough to throw into the conversation. An interpretation built on mere personal views is not really an interpretation, but speculation. It is the equivalent of trying to interpret a foreign language by making sincere guesses. A valid interpretation would be built on some form of authority, developed from research rather than wishful guessing.

Bible is the Word of God in the truest sense, we can begin to map out a purpose and define the parameters of life in this universe and direct our souls to find their way back to the Creator. It is the in-between that sends us down a thousand different paths. Partially accepting the Bible reduces us to selective obedience. This does not result in solid truth; it only reveals our preferences.

Even then, it is not so cut-and-dried. Clearly, all kinds of factors must be taken into consideration. As mentioned before, we all have hidden agendas. Then, pride and the deceptive lens of our own intellects must be considered. Many things can send us off in dangerous directions. [3]

MOVED BY THE SPIRIT

However, let's consider this part of the path first. Let's take some time to stand at this fork in the road. This particular landmark seems important. Just what is this book? Is it the Word of God or not? From here on, what kind of map we're using will make all the difference in the world. Can the Bible guide us? Trying to find directions using a map that is somewhat accurate seems not much better than using one that is outright fictional.

If we accept the Bible's claim that "the sum of Your word is truth" (Psalm 119:160), then we face a challenging task. This means we cannot casually discard or overlook anything. Nothing is expendable, and everything in the book is somehow relevant.

One of the writers in the Bible sheds some light on the inspiration issue: "But know this first of all, that no prophecy of Scripture is a matter of one's own interpretation, for no prophecy was ever made by an act of human will, but men moved by the Holy Spirit spoke from God" (2 Peter 1:20-21). The Bible claims it is not merely a product of human collaboration. God acted on the writers through His Spirit. They were "moved" by Him to accomplish the Word. But that does not mean they were just emotionally moved.

---

3 Regardless of the countless facets of confusion we devise, the premise of a steadfast truth still stands. The Word of God is the Truth. This basic aspect of the Bible is essential to establish before approaching it with our clumsy intellects.

In another part of the Bible, a similar word for "moved" is used in a different situation. Paul was on a ship. It was being "moved" by a storm. "When the ship was caught in it, and could not face the wind, we gave way to it, and let ourselves be driven along" (Acts 27:15). The phrase "driven along" is *epherometha*. When 2 Peter describes men being "moved" by the Holy Spirit, the word is *pheromenoi*. They both come from the base form *phero*, which is used to describe carrying a burden, moving something quickly, or prompting someone's mind. There is a possible parallel here. As the ship was "moved" by the storm, the writers of the Bible were "moved" by the Spirit in a similar way.

Men were on board the ship. Under normal circumstances, these men would have been in complete control of the direction they went. However, the storm changed everything. When the storm arrived, it began to determine the course of the ship. The men on board were coherent and aware, but they were no longer running things. Regardless of any input they might have had, the ship traveled a new course until the storm was finished.

In the same way, the writers of the Bible were in complete control of what they said and what they wrote. However, when the Holy Spirit became directly involved, the arrangement changed. He determined the course. Just like those on board the ship, there was no reason for them to lose their coherence or their awareness. Regardless of their own ideas, their writing instruments traveled along the path determined by the Spirit.

If we accept the fact that the Bible is inspired, it is important we take the term as it is presented in the Bible. To offer a minimal version of this concept is to open the door to the intrusive tinkering. Just as Paul was essentially in submission to the ship, we too must submit to the reality that this book is set for a course that is not susceptible to any of our efforts to reroute it. God has set the sails. This ship is locked on course, and any passenger must relinquish his own will if he is hoping to remain on board.

QUESTIONS

1. What words mentioned in this chapter are often misunderstood because they are generally defined incorrectly? Can you think of other examples?

2. What does the word "inspiration" literally mean in the Bible?

3. Why is it important to distinguish the world's definition of "inspiration" from the biblical definition?

4. What does "plenary" mean?

5. Why might there be hesitation to refer to the Word of God as perfect?

6. Why might there be a tendency to consider the Bible as only partially inspired?

7. Why is 2 Timothy 3:16 an essential "fork in the road"?

8. What are the possible complications of considering the Bible to be only partially inspired?

9. Why might there be fewer complications if we consider the Bible to be completely inspired?

10. What does the ship mentioned in Acts 27 have to do with the concept of inspiration?

Chapter 3

WRITING
MATERIALS

Shepherds and kings and doctors and fishermen – these were the instruments God used. Each writer came from his own unique background, and each one played a significant part in recording God's will.

Although God inspired these men to write down what He wanted, their individual personalities came through. Revelation would have been written differently if Jeremiah had written it instead of John. The Gospel of Luke would have had a different style and tone if written by David. Solomon used poetry. Paul used sports metaphors. Each writer's "voice" is apparent. God inspired them, but that does not mean He shut them down, bypassed their personalities, and used only their writing hand. He used their minds and their circumstances as well. He used a specific person for each specific message.

Any writer might select a pen rather than a pencil. He might decide to use a pen with black ink rather than one with blue ink. When he puts his thoughts down on paper, which tool he used will be apparent. The "personality" of the writing utensil will be recognizable. But that does not mean the tool had any say-so about any of the words. The pen is mightier than the sword, but the pen is certainly not mightier than the author.

It is also important to keep in mind that the One who authored these books also authored these writers. Before David was born, God was distinctly aware of him (Psalm 139:13-16). The same is true of Jeremiah (Jeremiah 1:5). The same is true of every other person who ever lived. Not even the sparrows fly under God's radar (Matthew 10:29). God knew the dimensions of the lives of His writers even before they were born. He knew every facet of their circumstances – the ones He would use to fashion them as well as what they wrote – even before He spoke the world into existence. Their personalities, freewill choices and all were thoroughly known long before God inspired these men. It was not that God browsed through the world looking for someone who might generally suit His purpose. From the beginning, He arranged for the perfect tools to be among His supplies at the perfect time.

THE AUTHOR

The writers themselves made their own limited positions clear. They were not just jotting down their own personal thoughts. None of them was self-appointed. The Bible was never intended to be a commentary by man. It is nothing less than communication from the Creator. When it comes to Scripture, this has always been the case.

The Bible is filled with phrases, such as "Thus says the LORD," that consistently point to God as the Author. At the very least, the writers were convinced the words came from God.

David wrote, "The Spirit of the LORD spoke by me, and His word was on my tongue" (2 Samuel 23:2). According to Jeremiah, God said to him, "Behold, I have put My words in your mouth" (Jeremiah 1:9). Paul went to great lengths to emphasize that his writings were not merely a human endeavor. He referred to himself as "Paul an apostle (not sent from men nor through the agency of man, but through Jesus Christ and God the Father, who raised Him from the dead)" (Galatians 1:1). He made it a point to clarify the true origins of his writings: "For I would have you know, brethren, that the gospel which was preached by me is not according to man. For I neither received it from man, nor was I taught it, but I received it through a revelation of Jesus Christ" (vv. 11-12). This was meant to remove any confusion about the source.

In another letter, Paul emphasized that his own personal abilities or lack thereof would have no effect on the message. It was important that his readers understood that "faith would not rest on the wisdom of men, but on the power of God" (1 Corinthians 2:5). Only the words of God Himself would serve as the foundation for faith.

THE INTEGRITY OF THE MESSAGE

Even if we assume an inspired writer was legitimate, there might be some concern about the reliability of his memory. If the truth was dependent on a man's "ready recollection," the Word of God might be unintentionally altered. However, God made arrangements to make sure His Word would not be a victim of anyone's forgetfulness. The Spirit of God would give the writer the words needed. "Do not worry about how or what you are to say; for it will be given you in that hour what you are to say. For it is not you who speak, but it is the Spirit of your Father who speaks in you" (Matthew 10:19-20). Whereas the human mind is often faulty and occasionally unreliable, the Spirit would secure the integrity of the message.

The writers of the New Testament were confident in the system of God's inspiration. When they referred to the books of the Old Testament, they did so without hesitation. The New Testament fully endorsed the divine nature of the Old Testament: "But know this first of all, that no prophecy of Scripture is a matter of one's own interpretation, for no prophecy was ever made by an act of human will, but men moved by the Holy Spirit spoke from God" (2 Peter 1:20-21). The key to a correct perspective of the Old Testament was the realization that the books were God's writings, not man's. Peter wrote that it was vital to "know this first of all" (v. 20) – clearly a priority assumption that had to be in place before proceeding any further.

Peter and John used David as a source. Referring to Psalm 2, they said: "By the Holy Spirit, through the mouth of our father David Your servant, said: 'Why did the Gentiles rage, and the peoples devise futile things? The kings of the earth took their stand, and the rulers were gathered together against the Lord and against His Christ' " (Acts 4:25-26). Peter and John did not consider David to be simply a quotable poet. They used these words as authoritative support because the words came "by the Holy Spirit, through the mouth of our father David Your servant" (v. 25).

Later in Acts, Paul did the same thing, but he made no distinction between what David said and what God said. David wrote: "For You will not abandon my soul to Sheol; nor will You allow Your Holy One to undergo decay' " (Psalm 16:10). When Paul referred to this passage, he considered it to be the very words of God: "He [God] also says in another Psalm, 'You will not allow Your Holy One to undergo decay' " (Acts 13:35). From the context, the pronoun "He" can be clearly identified as referring to God. This means that as far as Paul was concerned, the psalms were the words of God, not just the ramblings of a shepherd king.

This same approach to the Old Testament is found in the words of Jesus. In particular, His discussion with Satan reveals the Son of God's perspective concerning the writings of the Old Testament: "It is written, 'Man shall not live on bread alone, but on every word that proceeds out of the mouth of God' " (Matthew 4:4). In this particular instance, Jesus was quoting the writings of Moses. The passage, found in Deuteronomy, states:

> He humbled you and let you be hungry, and fed you with manna which you did not know, nor did your fathers know, that He might make you understand that man does not live by bread alone, but man lives by everything that proceeds out of the mouth of the LORD. (Deuteronomy 8:3)

These words were written by Moses, but Jesus treated them as if they were written by God. Jesus considered the words written by Moses to be inspired by God.

THE INTEGRITY OF THE NEW TESTAMENT

Even if the Old Testament is the inspired Word of God, there may be some who doubt whether the New Testament carries the same authority. Yet the New Testament claims that the things written by Luke, Paul and Peter are of the same caliber as the things written by Moses, Jeremiah and Malachi: "God, after He spoke long ago to the fathers in the prophets in many portions and in many ways, in these last days has spoken to us in His Son, whom He appointed heir of all things, through whom also He made the world" (Hebrews 1:1-2). This includes not only Jesus Himself, but also those who spoke what He revealed to them, which is just as Paul said, "I received it through a revelation of Jesus Christ" (Galatians 1:12). The New Testament is just as inspired as the Old Testament.

According to 2 Timothy 3:16, everything that can be identified as "Scripture" is inspired. Peter used the word "Scripture" to refer to the writings of Paul:

> Just as also our beloved brother Paul, according to the wisdom given him, wrote to you, as also in all his letters, speaking in them of these things, in which are some things hard to understand, which the untaught and unstable distort, as they do also the rest of the Scriptures. (2 Peter 3:15-16)

If the writings of Paul were considered "Scripture," then Paul was inspired. This means that anything in the Bible written by Paul is just as authoritative as anything from Genesis to Malachi.

A MESSAGE MADE MORE SURE

We might even consider the inspiration of the New Testament to be positioned on a higher level. One of the key differences is that the New Testament writers were dealing with the complete revelation of God's plan: "By referring to this, when you read you can understand my insight into the mystery of Christ, which in other generations was not made known to the sons of men, as it has now been revealed to His holy apostles and prophets in the Spirit" (Ephesians 3:4-5). What had been a mystery to the Old Testament writers was no longer a mystery. However, their ignorance of the big picture does not make their writing any less authoritative, because God's own mind was the source of their information. But their writing was only a shadow of what was to come. The full reality would be known only under the New Covenant. At this point, God's plan was fully expressed in a way that had never been done before. [1]

---

1 The essentially greater significance of the New Testament is emphasized in Hebrews 12:25.

Today, it seems that many people treat the New Testament like a mildly authoritative set of guidelines. The words delivered during the time of Jesus and shortly after His resurrection are the fulfillment of what was established in the Old Testament. Everything has been leading to what the New Testament writers would say – the culmination of God's Word.

God used Peter to drive this point home. Referring to the Transfiguration, Peter said:

> For we did not follow cleverly devised tales when we made known to you the power and coming of our Lord Jesus Christ, but we were eyewitnesses of His majesty. For when He received honor and glory from God the Father, such an utterance as this was made to Him by the Majestic Glory, "This is My beloved Son with whom I am well-pleased" – and we ourselves heard this utterance made from heaven when we were with Him on the holy mountain. So we have the prophetic word made more sure, to which you do well to pay attention as to a lamp shining in a dark place, until the day dawns and the morning star arises in your hearts. (2 Peter 1:16-19)

The information delivered during the Transfiguration was serious business. God was speaking directly to Peter and the others to confirm the divinity and authority of His Son. This event was also directly related to the "prophetic word" that was in the process of being delivered by the apostles. Their inspired message was "made more sure" by the literal voice of God on that particular day.

At the very least, the two testaments are treated as equals. In one particular passage, the seam fades completely. "For Scripture says, 'You shall not muzzle the ox while he is threshing,' and 'The laborer is worthy of his wages' " (1 Timothy 5:18). In one breath, this passage refers to Deuteronomy 25:4 and Luke 10:7. The words of God through Moses and through Luke are both identified as "Scripture."

PAUL'S OPINION

In his first letter to the Corinthians, Paul's comments about marriage were still within the jurisdiction of God's divine guidance. Paul blatantly stated, "I give an opinion" (7:25). The full phrase is "I give an opinion as one who by the mercy of the Lord is trustworthy" (v. 25). But later he also wrote, "I think that I also have the Spirit of God" (v. 40). He added, "If anyone thinks he is a prophet or spiritual, let him recognize that the things which I write to you are the Lord's commandment" (14:37). [2] Despite God allowing Paul to voice his opinion in the matter, it was an opinion allowed by inspiration. In this particular instance, Paul's perspective was given permission to surface within the authority of God. [3]

WRITTEN BY MEN, AUTHORED BY GOD

With all this in mind, it is reasonable at least to consider the possibility that these writers were lying. This is a legitimate hypothesis. However, all reliable external evidence indicates they were telling the truth. An internal examination reveals only integrity and an almost eerie unity throughout the books, suggesting a single Author despite the fact that the writers represent a wide variety of personalities and backgrounds.

Despite the evidence, there are some who might indeed conclude the writers are lying. But to suggest that these men were only partially telling the truth seems to be building a gray area that has no real support and serves no purpose. If these passages are merely the insightful suggestions of men and only men – if they were only eyewitnesses, if they were only religious teachers – it seems more than foolish to risk your soul on what they had to say. They themselves claim to be delivering the message of God. If this is not true, then they are either lying or confused.

If they were inspired by God, in the truest sense of the word, every book of the Bible must be taken seriously and no amount of modern tinkering can change the fact that all of them were authored by God.

---

2 The letter to the Corinthians is a crucial elaboration of the Old Covenant. God was using Paul to establish new considerations in keeping with the New Covenant. It seems highly unlikely that God would suddenly just let Paul "run loose" with opinions that He did not completely endorse.

3 It is also worth noting that Paul's comments concerning marriage were specifically dealing with the contemporary circumstances. "I think then that this is good in view of the present distress, that it is good for a man to remain as he is" (1 Corinthians 7:26). This does not mean that the situation was dictating the shape of the truth. God never allowed His Word to submit to man's ideas. But He did deal with specific situations that are no longer a factor (speaking in tongues, the destruction of Jerusalem, etc.).

QUESTIONS

1. Name some biblical writers who represent a wide range of backgrounds.

2. Why is God's omniscience relevant to the issue of the Bible being written by mere men?

3. What are some phrases in the Bible that indicate Scripture did not come from the minds of the writers only?

4. How was the Spirit's involvement in inspiration significant to the final result?

5. Why is it important that biblical writers quoted other biblical writers?

6. Why is it important that Jesus quoted biblical writers?

7. Why is it significant when a writing is identified as "Scripture"?

8. Why might the New Testament be considered a higher level of inspiration than the Old Testament?

9. How do we reconcile the presence of Paul's opinion found in Scripture, as mentioned in 1 Corinthians 7?

10. Why is it vital that the writers be thought of as more than simply eyewitnesses?

Chapter 4

FINAL SAY

T here is a difference between bickering and arguing. If someone simply raises his voice or repeats his side of the issue over and over, it usually means he is only bickering. This kind of thing does not necessarily require any kind of real thinking. The only requirement is volume and a blind devotion to an idea, regardless of the facts. This is of the same caliber as two kids involved in a dispute during a long road trip.

A rational argument requires thinking. It doesn't necessarily have to be loud and, in fact, can be strong without the decoration of bluster. A rational argument is built on a series of logical premises, not just the false security of stubborn repetition.

In this day and age, the majority of people seem to think that any opinion is valid just because it is an opinion. Prodded by radio talk shows and the open-range toleration of modern philosophy, we are under the impression that everybody's opinion matters. Whether or not it is based on fact, whether or not it is even based on logic, the current mindset holds to the idea that you don't have to build your ideas on anything but your own preferences.

However, a solid argument is distinct primarily in that it appeals to some source of authority. Even a child who is caught up in a backseat debate knows that if he believes he has a genuine shot at making his point, he must bring in the higher authority of those in the front seat – the parents. Their word is final, and the conflict of "stop touching me" or "make him stop doing that" is settled once and for all.

IT IS WRITTEN

Defenders of the truth in the Bible turned to Scripture as the highest authority. Faced with a dispute of any significance, they used Scripture to settle the argument. Considering the reaction of those involved, the implication was that Scripture had the kind of caliber that was irrefutable.

When faced with a skirmish over the truth, standard procedure for Paul was to use Scripture to salvage solid conclusions: "And according to Paul's custom, he went to them, and for three Sabbaths reasoned with them from the Scriptures" (Acts 17:2). Whenever there was a disagreement about something, God's words were used to settle the matter. When it came to conflicting concepts, one question in particular rose up to settle whatever matter was at hand: "What does the Scripture say?" (Romans 4:3). This moved the debate beyond simple opinion. The input of Scripture was the deciding factor. No wonder the phrase "it is written" is found extensively throughout the New Testament.

Paul and the rest of the apostles used the Word to build the truth because Jesus did the same. Despite the fact that Jesus had the authority of the voice of God "uttered" during the Transfiguration and despite the miracles that established His unlimited authority, Jesus used Scripture to settle arguments.

In the wilderness, when Jesus faced our common enemy, there were no blasts of energy. There was no wrestling match. It was a conversation. But make no mistake. Not only was the spiritual purity of Jesus on the line, but so were the souls of every one of us. If Jesus had sinned one time, He would have been disqualified as the perfect sacrifice, and the rescue of humanity would have failed.

During this crucial conflict, it was Scripture that saved the day. When Jesus was tempted to turn stone into bread, He reacted with "It is written" and referred to Deuteronomy 8:3: "Man shall not live on bread alone, but on every word that proceeds out of the mouth of God" (Matthew 4:4). When Satan twisted Scripture to serve his own purpose, Jesus said, "It is written," and He quoted Deuteronomy 6:16: "You shall not put the Lord your God to the test" (Matthew 4:7). When Satan tempted Jesus with power, Jesus said, "It is written," and He referred to Deuteronomy 6:13: "You shall worship the Lord your God, and serve Him only" (Matthew 4:10). Faced with the most dangerous enemy in existence, Jesus used Scripture to win. Anything less than inspired truth would have ended in defeat.

THE HIGHEST AUTHORITY

In order to face the same enemy – our adversary who manipulates and deceives – it is vital that we too are armed with the actual words of God. Our survival depends on it. A book of guidelines or generalizations would make us easy prey. But with the true authority of Scripture, we are also able to defy the enemy and all opponents of the truth.

Any time that Jesus was dealing with someone who attempted to undermine the truth, He used Scripture as the final say. When the Sadducees built their fantastical situation-ethics scenario involving a woman who was married sequentially to seven different men, Jesus dismantled their sophistry by pointing out a key flaw in their thinking: "You are mistaken, not understanding the Scriptures" (Matthew 22:29). The implication was that their grasp of the truth – in essence, their grasp of reality – was left wanting because they did not use Scripture to build their conclusions. The inevitable result was flawed thinking. [1]

In the turmoil of opinion, perspectives and interpretations, the words of God settled everything. Jesus, and even His apostles, had miracles as a badge of authority, but the Word was enough to get to the truth of the matter.

When Paul was in Berea, he found himself in the presence of people who were determined to know the truth. They listened to what Paul said, but their investigation did not stop there. Although they had an actual apostle standing in front of them, they went to the Scriptures every day to verify what he had told them: "Now these were more noble-minded than those in Thessalonica, for they received the word with great eagerness, examining the Scriptures daily to see whether these things were so"

---

1 The Pharisees also showed a basic misunderstanding by either ignoring or being ignorant of the truth (Matthew 19:3-8; 22:41-46).

(Acts 17:11). When it came to the truth, if you wanted to know if certain things were accurate, the touchstone was the Word of God.

UNBROKEN SCRIPTURE

Because the New Testament was in the process of being completed, these "Scriptures" were the books of the Old Testament. So in this case, the writings of the Old Testament were used to verify the authority of the New Testament. Because this was a search for truth, it was necessary that Scripture be involved. In the presence of all things potentially inconclusive, Scripture provided conclusions.

When the people of God referred to Scripture, there was never any indication that it should be "taken with a grain of salt." Clearly, we must always take into account the context and genre of each book. The apocalyptic symbolism of Daniel is not going to deliver the truth in the exact same way as the poetry of Psalms. But these considerations do not eliminate the authority of any Scripture.

For example, assaulted by excess analysis, the Proverbs are often treated as secondary truths reigned in by situation ethics or by our own sense of realism. When Peter referred to passages from Proverbs, he did not do this. As directed by God, Peter anchored a very significant point concerning those who fall away from the church, and he did it with the book of Proverbs (23:8): "It has happened to them according to the true proverb, 'A dog returns to its own vomit,' and 'A sow, after washing, returns to wallowing in the mire' " (2 Peter 2:22). There is no indication here that this was meant to be a loosely applied poem. If anything, used near the end of his argument, this was yet again God's inspired truth used as the final say in the matter. [2]

Nothing in the Bible suggests that any part of it is a lesser truth. When it comes to Scripture, all other sources must make adjustments. Although it is surrounded by numerous ideas and philosophies, the

---

2 At first glance, this passage of Scripture may appear to suggest that this verse in particular is a "true proverb," seemingly implying that other proverbs may not be true. This conclusion would ultimately lead to inevitable debates to determine which of the proverbs are true and which are not. The reality is so much more simple. Peter was just saying that the proverbs were proven to be true by the circumstances he was addressing. If anything, this phrase is an endorsement that implies that all the proverbs are just as true as the one being quoted.

Word of God does not bend to outside input. Many man-made arguments must reshape themselves when faced with higher authority, but Scripture is not malleable. As Jesus explained, "the Scripture cannot be broken" (John 10:35). It cannot be edited or undone by any higher authority because no such authority exists. In pursuit of the spiritual matters, all other works must yield.

This hard-and-fast nature of the Word is part of what makes it so powerful. Its plenary nature is vital in order to have any real say-so in matters of importance. To bring a "fuzzy" book into the arena would not help – it would only make the issues more confusing.

ATTENTION TO DETAIL

Scripture is not only true; it is specifically true. "Until heaven and earth pass away, not the smallest letter or stroke shall pass away from the Law until all is accomplished" (Matthew 5:18). This eliminates the idea that Scripture speaks in useful generalities.

When God commissioned Jeremiah to deliver His inspired message, God emphasized the details: "Stand in the court of the LORD's house, and speak to all the cities of Judah, who have come to worship in the LORD's house all the words that I have commanded you to speak to them. Do not omit a word!" (Jeremiah 26:2). To omit any part of the message would have been a failure on the part of Jeremiah as a messenger of God.

This same attention to detail can be seen in an argument Paul made. The issue at hand was balanced on a single word and whether this particular word was singular or plural: "Now the promises were spoken to Abraham and to his seed. He does not say, 'And to seeds,' as referring to many, but rather to one, 'And to your seed,' that is, Christ" (Galatians 3:16).

This reveals a basic assumption presumed by those who were directly involved with delivering the words of God. Scripture was considered to be an accurate source of authority down to the letter. God did not just deliver the gist of what He wanted. In order for the Bible to have any kind of input for matters of salvation, it was vital that it be reliable through and through. Nothing would be more effective at getting to the truth than the Word of God.

PERSUASIVE AND POWERFUL

This is clearly seen in the story Jesus told about a dead man. During his life in this world, the dead man had been rich, but in the existence that followed, he was not well-off at all. His condition was so miserable he hoped to warn his brothers who still lived so that they might avoid his own terrible situation. His plan was to send someone back from the dead to alert his brothers. Certainly a message delivered by a dead person would be enough to capture the attention of even the most callous soul. But this request was denied.

There was something better than a post-mortem sermon: "They have Moses and the Prophets; let them hear them" (Luke 16:29). The implication is that if you had the choice between delivering the truth via a resurrected dead person or the Word of God, the second option is suitable for the job. "If they do not listen to Moses and the Prophets, they will not be persuaded even if someone rises from the dead" (v. 31). We might think that a resurrection would be startling enough to convince people to focus on the spiritual realm. But it is the Word of God that will save the day. [3]

It is written that all Scripture is inspired. This same passage goes on to say that Scripture can be used for "teaching, for reproof, for correction, for training in righteousness" (2 Timothy 3:16). To be qualified as a tool for reproving or correcting, it would have to be a powerful authority. If it contains anything less than the words of God, it is not be suitable for correcting anything.

The Bible even goes so far as to claim the ability to judge the innermost part of us. Whereas human judgment must rely on appearances – empirical evidence and hopefully untainted examination – Scripture is able to appraise the very heart of a man: "For the Word of God is living and active and sharper than any two-edged sword, and piercing as far as the division of soul and spirit, of both joints and marrow, and able to judge the thoughts and intentions of the heart" (Hebrews 4:12). Nothing else is able to qualify for this kind of power on so many levels.

---

3 Certainly Jesus set our hope in motion by returning from the grave, but none of us have actually witnessed this event. "Blessed are they who did not see, and yet believed" (John 20:29). When it comes to closing the deal and having a final say on what really matters, it is the Word of God that convinces us that Jesus did come back from the dead.

The Bible is the highest authority. If necessary, all other works must step aside. If they are in opposition, all other ideas and philosophies must withdraw. We must see the Bible as this kind of presence. It is nothing less than a divine and perfect message. It is the authority by which all other judgments are judged.

QUESTIONS

1. How can you sometimes tell if someone does not have support for his or her argument?

2. In general, how much of public opinion is based on a rational argument?

3. Why does the phrase "it is written" show up so much in the New Testament?

4. Why is it significant that Jesus used Scripture to oppose Satan?

5. How is the true nature of the Word a vital issue concerning our own dealings with Satan?

6. What two characteristics of the Bereans show a clear perspective of the Word of God?

7. How do we know that such books as Psalms or Proverbs are just as authoritative as the rest of the Bible?

8. Why is the statement "Scripture cannot be broken" from John 10:35 so significant?

9. How do we know that Scripture is not just generally true but specifically true?

10. What does the story of the rich man and Lazarus reveal about Scripture (Luke 16)?

11. If the Bible is able to correct (2 Timothy 3:16) and judge (Hebrews 4:12), what does this tell us about the nature of the Bible?

Chapter 5

THE MOUTH
OF GOD

David executed a young man needlessly. The young man was an Amalekite who did himself in by lying. Although King Saul had committed suicide, the young man reported to David that he himself had actually killed the king, thinking he would be praised for dispatching David's enemy.

On the contrary, David was not happy. "Your blood is on your head, for your mouth has testified against you, saying, 'I have killed the LORD's anointed' " (2 Samuel 1:16). David ordered his men to kill the young man immediately.

It was the mouth. Although, in this case, it failed to represent the truth, the mouth testified against the young man, resulting in his early death. It was assumed that the young man's mouth told it like it was.

This kind of thinking is also found in the trial of Jesus. His words were truth, but that truth was offensive enough to those hearing Him that it resulted in His death. His accusers made it clear why they believed this case was closed: "What further need do we have of testimony? For we have heard it ourselves from His own mouth" (Luke 22:71).

It wasn't because of the look in His eyes or His body language. It was His mouth. Those present believed that the mouth was an accurate representative of a person.

A RELIABLE SYSTEM

For the most part, a man has control over his mouth. There are occasions when his mouth might betray him and hundreds of ways for his words to get tangled into meaningless or embarrassing phrases. We can all look back on other times and cringe, remembering how our anger or ignorance led us to say something foolish.

However, the majority of the time our mouths faithfully express what we want them to. If the mouth consistently failed in this respect, we would find another way of expressing ourselves.

Jesus indicated the mouth was more than suitable for measuring a person: "The good man out of the good treasure of his heart brings forth what is good; and the evil man out of the evil treasure brings forth what is evil; for his mouth speaks from that which fills his heart" (Luke 6:45). The mouth is not just a device that produces words; it is an audible version of the heart. [1]

Because the mouth speaks for the person, it carries a certain amount of authority. If this is true for man, this is likely to be also true for God. Anyone verified as God's "mouth" would accurately present the words of God's heart and mind. This means that any "mouth" of God would also carry authority.

It is safe to assume that any person who served as the mouth of God would have some reliability – at the very least, the same degree of reliability we count on when using our own mouths. Fashioned by the divine power of God (who uses even the free will of His creation to shape His plans), one might even conclude that when it comes to the mouth of God, regardless of human flaws, nothing will be tangled up or confused. God does not stutter.

There were several times when God assured the reader of His words that what had been written was an accurate delivery of what He wanted to say. One way of "sealing" the words to be delivered was by pointing

---

1 In Isaiah 6, the prophet was allowed a vision of the presence of God. The prophet's initial reaction was despair. Isaiah had a deep sense of being unworthy of God's presence, and he traced this shame back to his own mouth: "I am a man of unclean lips" (v. 5). In this vision, God purified Isaiah, and He did so by focusing on Isaiah's mouth (v. 7). This again indicates that the nature of man is strongly connected with his mouth and the words that are formed there.

out the fact it came from His own mouth. The message was sealed with the phrase "the mouth of the LORD has spoken" (Isaiah 1:20; 58:14; Micah 4:4). This implied that whoever received what had been spoken would treat the message as authority.

WORDS AND ACTIONS

In fact, the idea was that you better not interfere with what had come from God's mouth. His Word, as delivered, was so authoritative that it would be unwise to stand in its way. "So will My Word be which goes forth from My mouth; it will not return to Me empty, without accomplishing what I desire, and without succeeding in the matter for which I sent it" (Isaiah 55:11). When God spoke, it was expected that things would happen. Just as with us, God's mouth was expected to be strongly associated with His actions.

When a man's words do not match his actions, this usually means his integrity is in question. Such a conflict is a symptom of duplicity. The hands should be in correlation with the mouth. Solomon saw this integrity of words and action in God. In his prayer, Solomon said to God: "That which You have promised him; indeed You have spoken with Your mouth and have fulfilled it with Your hand as it is this day" (1 Kings 8:24). When it comes to people, words and actions do not always match, but when it comes to God, the unity of His purpose through what He says and what He does is flawless.

Whenever God spoke, He eventually followed that by acting on what He said: "I declared the former things long ago and they went forth from My mouth, and I proclaimed them. Suddenly I acted, and they came to pass" (Isaiah 48:3). The integrity of God's words and God's actions has always been intact.

DESTRUCTIVE AND CREATIVE

The mouth of God is associated with power and authority – the kind that defies any opposition. Several passages address this in stark images. Sometimes, it is expressed through the metaphor of fire: "His breath kindles coals, and a flame goes forth from His mouth" (Job 41:21). "Smoke went up out of His nostrils, and fire from His mouth devoured; coals were kindled by it" (Psalm 18:8). The mouth of God is potentially destructive, depending on the nature of those who hear it: "Behold, I am making My words in your mouth fire and this people wood, and it will consume them" (Jeremiah 5:14). Being on the flammable end of this analogy, we would all do well to take this description to heart.

In some places, the images are even more violent: "Therefore I have hewn them in pieces by the prophets; I have slain them by the words of My mouth" (Hosea 6:5). The same violent parallel is described in the New Testament as well: "Then that lawless one will be revealed whom the Lord will slay with the breath of His mouth and bring to an end by the appearance of His coming" (2 Thessalonians 2:8). After this, the almost surreal imagery found toward the end of God's Word is no surprise: "Therefore repent; or else I am coming to you quickly, and I will make war against them with the sword of My mouth" (Revelation 2:16). [2] To oppose such authority would be foolish and dangerous. There is no indication in Scripture that the mouth of God – whoever or whatever might have been representing it – produced anything less than this kind of authority.

The destructive nature of this authority is also accompanied by its power to create. When God created the universe out of nothing, God chose to speak it into existence: "By the word of the LORD the heavens were made, and by the breath of His mouth all their host" (Psalm 33:6). Just as the words from the mouth of God can mean destruction for those who oppose Him, His words are also nothing less than life for those who turn to Him:

> He humbled you and let you be hungry, and fed you with manna which you did not know, nor did your fathers know, that He might make you understand that man does not live by bread alone, but man lives by everything that proceeds out of the mouth of the LORD. (Deuteronomy 8:3)

Whereas the mouth of God is a sword of retribution or a blazing fire that means certain doom for the world, it is also our very sustenance. Job realized this: "I have not departed from the command of His lips; I have treasured the words of His mouth more than my necessary food" (Job 23:12). One way or the other, the mouth of God determines our survival.

---

2 See also Revelation 1:16.

AUTHORIZED WORDS

If His hearers are so dependent on His words, He would certainly make sure that any vessel of delivery He selected would be a secure one. God chose specific people to be His mouth, and at no point did He ever indicate they would be iffy messengers:

> I will raise up a prophet from among their countrymen like you, and I will put My words in his mouth, and he shall speak to them all that I command him. It shall come about that whoever will not listen to My words which he shall speak in My name, I Myself will require it of him. But the prophet who speaks a word presumptuously in My name which I have not commanded him to speak, or which he speaks in the name of other gods, that prophet shall die. (Deuteronomy 18:18-20)

The message was so important that any tampering with it by even the messenger himself would cost him his life. To speak on behalf of God without having His full endorsement was a serious offense.

All in all, God apparently believed that this method of communication was more than suitable. "I have put My words in your mouth" (Isaiah 51:16). "Behold, I have put My words in your mouth" (Jeremiah 1:9). "God spoke by the mouth of His holy prophets from ancient time" (Acts 3:21). As far as He was concerned, His "mouth" would say only what He wanted to say.

Not everyone was qualified for such an honor. Anyone who showed lack of respect for God's words was rejected: "But to the wicked God says, 'What right have you to tell of My statutes and to take My covenant in your mouth?' For you hate discipline and you cast My words behind you'" (Psalm 50:16-17). There was a clear distinction between the one who was authorized to speak as the mouth of God and those who were speaking from their own minds: "Do not listen to the words of the prophets who are prophesying to you. They are leading you into futility; they speak a vision of their own imagination, not from the mouth of the LORD" (Jeremiah 23:16). [3] The Bible contains the words as delivered

---

3 See also Jeremiah 14:14.

by the mouth of God. Even when God allowed Job's friends to express freely their deep lack of wisdom, any non-truth was clearly identified as such before the book of Job was brought to a close (Job 42:7-8).

CHAIN OF COMMUNICATION

There was one point in history when the arrangement would have seemed the most precarious. It was also a time when vital information had to be delivered accurately from God to man. Anything less than exact obedience could have meant death. Yet the chain of communication was unusually long. In most situations, God gave His message to a man who then spoke to the people. In this particular case, the line of communication was extended.

Moses was uptight about being the guy who spoke directly to the people. Patient with these insecurities, God arranged for Aaron to be the actual public speaker instead. From an earthly perspective, this might seem to be a fragile system. After all, the more individuals involved, the more likely the message could be intentionally or inadvertently corrupted. Like the old game known as "Telephone" (aka "Gossip"), the words are vulnerable to corruption. The end result is rarely identical to the original.

Plus, Moses was under a great deal of pressure. When you are in charge of a disgruntled nation, there is going to be some stress. Is there not the possibility he might have gotten something wrong? Added something? Missed something?

What if Aaron had not heard Moses exactly right? A couple million refugees can cause a significant amount of background noise. What if Aaron had not quite caught everything his brother had said? It happens all the time. Every day, we experience how easy it is to fail to communicate. We are quite aware that language is susceptible to a thousand different species of confusion.

Despite all this, God arranged for this situation: the primary communication was given to Moses. "Now then go, and I, even I, will be with your mouth, and teach you what you are to say" (Exodus 4:12). Due to Moses' hesitation about public speaking, God added the extra link of Aaron. "You are to speak to him [Aaron] and put the words in his mouth; and I, even I, will be with your mouth and his mouth, and I will teach you what you are to do" (v. 15). From God to Moses to Aaron to the people – God did not hesitate at all with this chain.

There was no flaw in the line of communication because the same security system was being used: "Moreover, he shall speak for you to the people; and he will be as a mouth for you and you will be as God to him" (v. 16). In this passage, God was not only endorsing the setup He used, but He also shed light with an analogy.

In the analogy, Moses was God, and Aaron was God's mouth. Aaron, in essence, was Moses' prophet: "Then the LORD said to Moses, 'See, I make you as God to Pharaoh, and your brother Aaron shall be your prophet' " (Exodus 7:1). The implication is that the "mouth" will successfully deliver what God wants to be delivered – no more, no less. Despite Moses' insecurities, despite the extra link in the chain, nothing was lost as it moved through the system. [4]

THE BALAAM COMPLICATION

There was even one occasion when the "mouth" of God had plenty of strong reasons not to proclaim exactly what God wanted proclaimed. Balaam was hired as a kind of spiritual hit man. Balak saw the people of God as a real threat, so he approached Balaam, wanting him to curse the Israelites. It would be something along the lines of an assassination with a high-powered rifle.

Right from the start, Balaam tried to explain that it was not that simple. When it came to the power of the Word, if there was ever a conflict of interest, the authority was held only by God, and God's plans always superseded all other plans. "So Balaam said to Balak, 'Behold, I have come now to you! Am I able to speak anything at all? The word that God puts in my mouth, that I shall speak" (Numbers 22:38). Balaam would indeed wield the powerful words of God, but Balaam's own personal angle would be ignored. God, not Balak, would be the One who determined exactly what Balaam said. "Then the LORD put a word in Balaam's mouth and said, 'Return to Balak, and you shall speak thus' " (23:5). Regardless of Balak's military agenda, God's Word survived untainted.

---

4 A similar chain of people is found in Jeremiah 36. God spoke to Jeremiah, who spoke to Baruch, who wrote God's words down on a scroll. Then, Jehudi obtained the scroll and read it to the king. If the king's response is any indication, then the truth was successfully delivered.

Balaam actually ended up proclaiming the exact opposite of what his client wanted. When Balak angrily confronted his hit man, the prophet again tried to make the situation clear. "He replied, 'Must I not be careful to speak what the LORD puts in my mouth?' " (Numbers 23:12). It did not matter what Balak wanted. It did not matter what Balaam wanted. The only thing that mattered was what God wanted.

As long as Balaam served as God's mouth, he was strictly limited in what he could proclaim as the Word of God. When Balak still pushed for his agenda, God directed Balaam again to try and clarify. "Then the LORD met Balaam and put a word in his mouth and said, 'Return to Balak, and thus you shall speak' " (Numbers 23:16). Balaam tried to illuminate Balak concerning anyone who served as the mouth of God. "Balaam replied to Balak, 'Did I not tell you, "Whatever the Lord speaks, that I must do"?' " (v. 26). You would think this had settled the matter once and for all.

Sadly enough, this did not settle it as far as Balak was concerned. He took Balaam up to a high position so he could aim his curse better. When Balaam was in position, "the Spirit of God came upon him" (Numbers 24:2). And Balaam once again blessed the Israelites.

This made Balak very angry. "I called you to curse my enemies, but behold, you have persisted in blessing them these three times!" (Numbers 24:10). Balaam explained that no amount of money would change anything:

> Did I not tell your messengers whom you had sent to me, saying, "Though Balak were to give me his house full of silver and gold, I could not do anything contrary to the command of the LORD, either good or bad, of my own accord. What the LORD speaks, that I will speak"? (vv. 12-13)

In this particular instance, a whole array of obstacles stood in the path of the Word of God, yet it reached the other side unscathed. [5]

We too can be confident that the words of God have survived any man-made complications. If God chose someone as His mouth, you can

---

5 Also consider that God used Caiaphas, a man serving as high priest in a corrupt system, to prophesy about the imminent crucifixion of Jesus (John 11:51). See also the circumstances of the "old prophet" who is forced to oppose his previous lies (1 Kings 13:18-22). Both of these men had agendas that were in direct opposition to God, yet this did not prevent the divine message from being delivered.

rest assured that this appointed person spoke only what God wanted him to speak. Anything that came from the "mouth" of God was untainted by inner conflict or outside influence: "All the utterances of my mouth are in righteousness; there is nothing crooked or perverted in them" (Proverbs 8:8). No matter the general turmoil of the world. When God spoke, His message was delivered loud and clear.

QUESTIONS

1. How is the spoken word used today in a binding or authoritative way?

2. What connection is there between our hearts and the things we say?

3. Why is it significant when someone is referred to by God as His "mouth"?

4. Why is it important that a person's words and actions not be in conflict with one another?

5. How is the Word of God like fire?

6. How is the Word of God like a sword?

7. How is the Word of God like food?

8. How were God's communication arrangements with Moses more complicated than those at other times? What does this arrangement tell us about the integrity of God's messages to mankind?

9. How were God's communication arrangements with Balaam more complicated than those at other times? What does this arrangement tell us about the integrity of God's messages to mankind?

Chapter 6

THE VOICE
OF GOD

T he mountain was frightening. Everyone gathered at Mount Sinai was scared. It wasn't like watching a storm front move in.
It wasn't just an impressive cumulonimbus cloud. Anyone who was
there would not have mistaken it for simply grim weather. Something
unusual was going on.

There were thunder and lightning flashes, a thick cloud, and a very
loud trumpet sound (Exodus 19:16). [1] The sights and sounds were
such that "all the people who were in the camp trembled" (v. 16).
These were not doe-eyed simpletons. Keep in mind, counted among
the trembling were experienced soldiers. These grown men, who had
most recently fought and defeated the Amalekites (which certainly
involved some gruesome deaths and impromptu amputations), stood
before Sinai shaking in their sandals.

---

1 The trumpet within the context of the Bible is not normally associated with any kind
of pleasant or catchy music. This instrument was more often connected with a warning,
an announcement, or a call to arms. To us it would be something more along the lines of
a deafening alarm. The Sinai trumpet was probably not melodious, for such things do not
inspire fear. This was more than likely loud and frightening.

There's more. Smoke (not just clouds) billowed from the mountain. This was because the mountain was on fire. "Now Mount Sinai was all in smoke because the LORD descended upon it in fire; and its smoke ascended like the smoke of a furnace" (Exodus 19:18). Later, Moses wrote, "The mountain was burning with fire" (Deuteronomy 5:23). This was no overcast peak. The summit was in flames.

In addition to all this, "the whole mountain quaked violently" (Exodus 19:18). Like the people who stood nearby, the mountain itself trembled as if in fear.

No Hollywood rendition could capture the essence of this event. Computer-generated imagery alone would not create the appropriate awe. God was barely touching the world, and the result was nearly catastrophic. The people were in extreme danger. God told Moses to warn the people, "so that they do not break through to the LORD to gaze, and many of them perish" (Exodus 19:21). As it was, the people were in close enough proximity to be killed outright by the presence of God.

And then God spoke.

He started delivering His commandments with His own voice. The Ten Commandments were only the first of many commandments, but He paused after number 10. The people began pleading for some other arrangement:

> All the people perceived the thunder and the lightning flashes and the sound of the trumpet and the mountain smoking; and when the people saw it, they trembled and stood at a distance. Then they said to Moses, "Speak to us yourself and we will listen; but let not God speak to us, or we will die." (Exodus 20:18-19)

Per their request, Moses acted as the middleman, dealing with God face to face and then delivering God's words to the people (via Aaron). This is how the people wanted it. It wasn't just because God's voice made them uneasy. They were afraid the voice of God would kill them.

A VOICE OF POWER

As the mountain burned and shook, no one questioned the authority of the message. God's voice was the Law. Even God's voice through

Moses was the Law. Whether it was delivered through Moses or through Moses and then Aaron, it was the Law. If it was delivered through the songs of David, the voice of Jeremiah, or the letters of Paul, the voice of God meant authority.

His voice is power. Whether a matter of pure decibels or tone, when God spoke, there was a reaction. This has always been the case. When He created the universe, He did not sculpt the earth, He did not forge the stars, and He did not stir up the galaxies. He did not fashion or construct. He simply spoke: "Then God said, 'Let there be light'; and there was light" (Genesis 1:3). He spoke the physical realm into existence and then talked to it, and the response was expressed in continents and oceans and every form of life that moved in them: "Let the waters teem with swarms of living creatures, and let birds fly above the earth" (v. 20). Paul explained that God "calls into being that which does not exist" (Romans 4:17). When God spoke, there was always a response. Working with no previous material, His Word made everything out of nothing. The only ingredients were His will and His voice.

The same voice was the subject of one of David's songs: "The voice of the LORD is powerful, the voice of the LORD is majestic. The voice of the LORD breaks the cedars; yes, the LORD breaks in pieces the cedars of Lebanon" (Psalm 29:4-5). Whether the voice is creating or destroying, it is never doubted as powerful. All existence and life are balanced on His words. This is yet another facet of the fact that man lives by "every word that proceeds out of the mouth of God" (Matthew 4:4).

THE VOICE OF JESUS

So it's no wonder that Jesus was able to converse with the weather. For the One who created, it is not any more difficult to control what has been created. When Jesus was in a boat that was being bullied by a storm, He had a one-way dialogue with the elements. He "rebuked the wind and said to the sea, 'Hush, be still.' And the wind died down and it became perfectly calm" (Mark 4:39). The voice that said, "Hush, be still," was the same voice that said, "Let there be light" (Genesis 1:3). All matter acknowledges this sovereignty.

The voice of Jesus was the voice of God, so it had the same power. When the Great Physician approached the tomb of Lazarus, the patient had been dead for four days. There was no respiration, no pulse, and no brainwave activity. When Jesus took on this hopeless case, He did not resuscitate in any manner that we might have expected. He did not do CPR or place his hands on him to administer a bolt of lightning to revive the inert body. Jesus did not even go inside the tomb. "He cried out with a loud voice, 'Lazarus, come forth' " (John 11:43). And there was a response. "The man who had died came forth" (v. 44). Jesus simply spoke Lazarus back to life. It was the voice of God, and the voice of God is power. It is enough to wake the dead.

For those who die in Christ, although the last thing they will hear before they die will vary, the first thing they will hear after they die is the voice of Jesus: "Truly, truly, I say to you, an hour is coming and now is, when the dead will hear the voice of the Son of God, and those who hear will live" (John 5:25). [2] When you are dealing with the voice of Jesus, you are dealing with the voice of God. He is the God "who gives life to the dead" (Romans 4:17). That is the kind of power and authority involved when God speaks.

TWO MOUNTAINS

This power and authority are no less significant to the modern Christian. In the book of Hebrews, God made an analogy to emphasize the correct perspective. He compared two mountains – Sinai (representing the Old Covenant) and Zion (representing the New Covenant):

> For you have not come to a mountain that can be touched and to a blazing fire, and to darkness and gloom and whirlwind, and to the blast of a trumpet and the sound of words which sound was such that those who heard begged that no further word be spoken to them. (Hebrews 12:18-19)

Here, God revisited the intimidating environment of Sinai, assuring us that our situation is different than what the Israelites experienced:

> But you have come to Mount Zion and to the city of the living God, the heavenly Jerusalem, and to myriads of angels, to the general assembly and church of the firstborn who are

2 See also John 5:28-29.

enrolled in heaven, and to God, the Judge of all, and to the
spirits of the righteous made perfect, and to Jesus, the me-
diator of a new covenant, and to the sprinkled blood, which
speaks better than the blood of Abel. (vv. 22-24)

Everything has changed through fulfillment. We are dealing with
the same God, but we are under a different covenant. We are standing
before a different mountain.

A quick glance at this contrast between Sinai and Zion might seem to
suggest that the modern Christian is involved in a covenant that is not as
"serious" as Sinai. After all, we are not faced with a mountain that looks
like it is on the verge of exploding. It is easy to think of Zion as more
easygoing and casual – maybe the equivalent of a peaceful mountain on
a clear spring evening. However, the rest of this passage makes it clear
that this is not the case: "See to it that you do not refuse Him who is
speaking. For if those did not escape when they refused him who warned
them on earth, much less will we escape who turn away from Him who
warns from heaven" (Hebrews 12:25). The situation at Sinai was dead
serious, and God's commands were taken seriously. Lives were in the
balance depending on how the people responded to those commands.

The point of the passage is this: If Sinai was a big deal, Zion is a big-
ger deal. To suggest the New Testament is some kind of mild upgrade
with soft edges is a significant misunderstanding of God's Word. Things
have not been ramped down or cushioned. If anything, the volume has
been turned up. "And His voice shook the earth then, but now He has
promised, saying, 'Yet once more I will shake not only the earth, but
also the heaven' " (Hebrews 12:26). We now live in a time where the
voice of God has even deeper repercussions than ever before.

THE UTTERANCE

It meant something when the voice of God was heard during the
baptism of Jesus: "And behold, a voice out of the heavens said,
'This is My beloved Son, in whom I am well-pleased" (Matthew
3:17). [3] He wasn't just adding commentary. God was establishing
the authority of His Son. This man who was being immersed in

---

3 See also Mark 1:11; Luke 3:22.

water by John was not just another prophet. He was not just another teacher. This was God in flesh and blood, and God used His voice to make sure this was clear.

One of the few other times in the New Testament when God audibly spoke was during the Transfiguration. It was noticeably similar to the time He spoke up during the baptism of Jesus: "A bright cloud overshadowed them, and behold, a voice out of the cloud said, 'This is My beloved Son, with whom I am well-pleased; listen to Him!' " (Matthew 17:5). [4] Again, the issue at hand was authority. Jesus was not just another Moses. Jesus was not just another Elijah. He was so much more, and the world would be wise to pay attention.

Possibly a less familiar time when God literally spoke from heaven was when Jesus was speaking about His impending death and His own personal fear about it. "Now my soul has become troubled; and what shall I say, 'Father, save Me from this hour'? But for this purpose I came to this hour. Father, glorify Your name" (John 12:27-28). Jesus described His two choices, concerning what waited for Him on a cross outside Jerusalem. He could either ask God to rescue Him, or He could go through with it. He announced His decision. This was when God spoke up again: "Then a voice came out of heaven: 'I have both glorified it, and will glorify it again' " (v. 28). This conversation seems moot because Jesus is God in the flesh, and Jesus is speaking with God. But Jesus explained the purpose for the conversation: "This voice has not come for My sake, but for your sakes" (v. 30). The voice of God spoke up for the sake of those who were standing there. They needed to hear the voice of God.

When it came time for the New Covenant to be established, it was important there be no question about the authority of the New Covenant. When God speaks directly to the world, the world should sit up and take notice. The "utterance" during the Transfiguration was more than just an attention-getter (2 Peter 1:16-21). It was to emphasize that everything ultimately included in the New Testament would be given the same respect and attention as the Old Testament.

---

4 See also Mark 9:7; Luke 9:35.

NOTHING LESS

The authority of God's voice is supported right up to the end of the Bible. When John wrote down Revelation, he claimed to have been dealing with nothing less than "the voice which I heard from heaven" (Revelation 10:8). [5] The voice in Genesis that spoke creation into existence and the voice that delivered the apocalyptic vision to John are the same voice with the same authority.

A Christian recognizes the Bible (Old and New Testament) for what it is – the voice of God. This is one of the defining characteristics of a Christian: that he be able to know this voice. "The sheep follow him because they know his voice" (John 10:4). When it comes to having the truth, the Christian hears God's voice. "Everyone who is of the truth hears My voice" (18:37). Not just the audible version that once spoke on a mountain, but the one you find on the pages of the Bible. [6]

Our response is vital. "Today if you hear His voice, do not harden your hearts" (Hebrews 4:7). [7] Turning your back on the voice of God as recorded in the pages of the Bible or suggesting that it is something less than the voice of God seems to be nothing less than hardening your heart against it. Undermining the authority of the Bible is resistance to its true nature.

Through the centuries, God has used different means to deliver His message. When the people heard the voice of God at Sinai, they fully understood that they were dealing with God Himself and His authority. When the same voice made itself known through Moses and Aaron, it was still nothing less than the voice of God. When that voice spoke through the prophets or angels, it was still nothing less

---

5 See also Revelation 11:12; 12:10; 14:2, 13; 18:4.

6 Today, there are many who claim that the words of God can still be derived from sources other than the Bible. Whether through dreams, events, or outright audible messages, it is often suggested that God has communicated in various ways. Hebrews 1:1-2 seems a clear opposition to this idea. Providence is certainly a reality, but seeking for specific, non-biblical input from God is first of all potentially a form of neglect toward what God has already delivered through the Bible and also the perfect setup for all kinds of self-deception and self-endorsement ultimately leading back to our own wishes and desires.

7 See also Hebrews 3:7-8, 15.

than the voice of God. When the voice spoke through the flesh and blood of Jesus, it was still nothing less than the voice of God.

Now, the voice uses paper and ink. But it is nothing less than the voice of God.

QUESTIONS

1. What elements made Sinai frightening?

2. Why do you think God chose to speak creation into existence?

3. What possible connection is there between creation and Jesus calming the storm?

4. Why is it significant that Jesus simply spoke in order to raise Lazarus from the dead?

5. What indications are there today that some people think of the New Testament as "lesser" in comparison to the Old Testament?

6. What does the comparison of Sinai and Zion in Hebrews indicate about the seriousness of the New Covenant?

7. Why is it so important that God spoke when Jesus was baptized?

8. Why did Jesus pray out loud to God if, in essence, Jesus is God?

9. Why is it so important that God spoke at the Transfiguration?

10. How is the Bible just like the voice of God?

Chapter 7

THE BREATH
OF GOD

M oses was familiar with danger. His first nursery was the shallows of the Nile (Exodus 2:3). Years later, he killed an Egyptian and hid the body (v. 12). Shortly after that, he ventured off into unfamiliar territory and took on a group of shepherds single-handedly (v. 17). This was the same man who was terrified of public speaking.

Stand up in front of a group of people and give a speech? Absolutely not. Engage in mortal combat? No problem.

Whether Moses had an adventurous spirit might be debatable. But he sure seemed to have at least some bold curiosity one particular day. He asked if he could see God.

At this point in the journey toward the Promised Land, there had been multiple demonstrations of God's power. The 10 plagues, the parting of the Red Sea, not to mention the near-annihilation of Mount Sinai – all had strongly indicated that to interact with God was a precarious undertaking. Yet Moses presented his request: "I pray You, show me Your glory" (Exodus 33:18). Regardless of whether he knew it, this would be the most dangerous thing he had ever done.

God warned him: "You cannot see My face, for no man can see Me and live" (Exodus 33:20). In other instances, God had presented

Himself in, so to speak, survivable doses. But a true interaction with the Creator would destroy Moses.

So God made arrangements: "I will put you in the cleft of the rock and cover you with My hand until I have passed by. Then I will take My hand away and you shall see My back, but My face shall not be seen" (Exodus 33:22-23). Moses would catch a glimpse of God, and as an added bonus, he would survive the glimpse.

We often sing the song about "the cleft of the rock," but we probably don't fully appreciate the significance of what was going on that particular day. Moses was in the equivalent of a bunker and was covered with the hand of God. Then he saw the back of God. The hand of God kept Moses protected from the rest of God.

But God isn't a physical being (John 4:24). Physical material is temporary and fragile. God is spiritual. How could He have had a "hand" to cover Moses and then allowed Moses to see His "back"?

Many instances in the Bible describe God as if He has physical characteristics. Referring to the rainbow, God said, "I will look upon it" (Genesis 9:16). He told Hezekiah, "I have heard your prayer" (Isaiah 38:5). The clouds were described as "the dust beneath His feet" (Nahum 1:3).

If God is not a physical being, how can He see, hear and walk?

THE ESSENTIAL FACTOR

God can see, but He has no eyes. God can walk, but He has no feet. God can hear, but He has no ears. At least not in the physical sense. He is not a physical being. But when it comes to learning about the aspects of God, He often used physical terms to help define His nature.

Inspiration literally means "God-breathed." Although God does not have lungs, He does breathe. Because there are numerous other physical characteristics He could have used to express this idea, it is extremely important to consider the significance of why He would choose the concept of breathing in particular to portray how He would convey the Truth.

Because God is completely omnipotent, even as He designed the human body and constructed the respiratory system, He certainly had the concept of inspiration in mind. Each breath we take then is an appropriate reminder of how He chose to "breathe" His Word for us. Throughout Scripture, the theme of the "breath of life" emphasizes not only our trust in the authority of God's Word, but also our absolute dependence on it for our survival.

When creating the first human being, God did so with a purpose. Even the material He used to construct Adam would set up resounding themes. Man was made from dust, held together merely by the will of God. Man would live out his days inside a vessel that would ultimately return to its former components. But these basic materials alone were not enough. Regardless of the modern laboratory wannabes trying to quantify the mortal spark, you need life to make life.

Even when Adam's skeleton, circulatory system and brain were all in place, he was still unfinished. At this point, he was pretty much glorified dirt. Only when God gave Adam His own breath, did Adam begin to live: "Then the LORD God formed man of dust from the ground, and breathed into his nostrils the breath of life; and man became a living being" (Genesis 2:7). God's breath transformed the inanimate into the animate – the inorganic into the organic. The breath of God was the essential ingredient.

SUSTAINED

Not only must life originate from God, but it must also be maintained by God. Our investigation of matter has revealed that we are truly vapor, not only in duration but also in our basic components. Within the spinning system of each atom, there is a disturbing amount of empty space. The universe, the world, and even our very selves are primarily a complex manipulation of particles whirling around vast nothings. We are ghosts made of flesh. Through His Son, God sustains the vapor of this realm: "In Him all things hold together" (Colossians 1:17). As we peel back layer after layer of this existence, it is easy to imagine the subquantum forces as fingerprints of the Creator who is constantly keeping His creation from becoming uncreated.

Whether any living thing continues to breathe is completely dependent on God: "Who among all these does not know that the hand of the LORD has done this, in whose hand is the life of every living thing, and the breath of all mankind?" (Job 12:9-10). [1] Just as we need to breathe

---

1 See also Job 33:4; Daniel 5:23.

constantly to live, we must rely on God's own breath to continue to live. When faced with the precariousness of this existence, those who belonged to God knew very well who determined its durability.

When Paul addressed the manic idolatry of Athens, one of his first points was to remind the Athenians of the life force that only God controlled: "He Himself gives to all people life and breath and all things" (Acts 17:25). This distinguished the true God from all the false gods that infected the Athenian landscape. The true God had the power of the breath of life.

GOD SPOKE

When God designed the human body, He also came up with a pretty amazing contraption that could produce speech. Like the ultimate Rube Goldberg device, the lungs, vocal cords, teeth and tongue interact with each other in complex patterns to form sounds that can be interpreted into meaning. We take it for granted, but it really is an amazing system.

When God created the universe, He spoke. But He does not use any of the basic contraptions needed to produce actual speech, which might be extremely significant. The voice of God is certainly an audible event, but His speech is not dependent on the interaction of the standard physical components we depend on. He could have chosen any other method. When He began to create, He could have waved his "hands" or stomped His "feet." But when the Creator created, He spoke: "By the word of the LORD the heavens were made, and by the breath of His mouth all their host" (Psalm 33:6). The breath of God would not just be associated with providing the spark of life. It would also be associated with words – and in His case, words of power.

This might explain why God pointed out certain shortcomings of idols: "They have ears, but they do not hear, nor is there any breath at all in their mouths" (Psalm 135:17). [2] Bringing to our attention the fact that idols lack respiration might not have been just a matter of stating the obvious. It might have been a reminder that these man-made gods were clearly no source of life and were certainly

---

2 See also Jeremiah 10:14; 51:17; Habakkuk 2:19.

incapable of having any authority over creation. It seems likely this is why Paul provided the same contrast right away with the Athenians. It was important they knew the difference between the God who could breathe and the breathless tokens that littered their city.

THE BONES

Because the breath of God is what determines life, it is easy to see why it is also involved in judgment. Those who defy the Creator with their lives will lose their lives: "With the breath of His lips He will slay the wicked" (Isaiah 11:4). It is a great foolishness to oppose the One who gives you your very breath.

The breath of God is death for those who reject Him. But for those who seek God, it is life. This was made obvious to Ezekiel, who, in a vision, found himself in the middle of a valley of death. God put Ezekiel there to show him something incredibly important. It was a scene that would be gruesome for most: "The hand of the LORD was upon me, and He brought me out by the Spirit of the LORD and set me down in the middle of the valley; and it was full of bones" (Ezekiel 37:1). Just bones – lots of them. Some assembly would be required.

There was no life. There was only death. To emphasize just how dead these bones were, the Scripture tells us "they were very dry" (Ezekiel 37:2). A little glint of blood might have been a sign of hope, but this would be starting from scratch. God placed Ezekiel among these lifeless bones and then asked a question: "Can these bones live?" (v. 3). When faced with only a semblance of life – the basic pieces, essentially only the memory of life – what can be done to recover anything? How can you bring to life something that is so beyond rescue?

But God used Ezekiel to bring the bones back to life. It was a mass resurrection. To accomplish this incredible feat, God did not have Ezekiel sort through the pile of skeletal debris. The solution was powerful, but simple. God told Ezekiel to "prophesy over these bones" (Ezekiel 37:4). In other words, Ezekiel used the Word.

Concerning this lifeless landscape of bones, God delivered a message through Ezekiel: "Behold, I will cause breath to enter you that you may come to life" (Ezekiel 37:5). When Ezekiel delivered the prophecy, this was the very breath of God, and this, in turn, resulted in life.

When Ezekiel began to speak the words of God, the bones began to rattle and come together. This was not just to provide the means for a catchy folk song ("the foot bone's connected to the leg bone"). God was making a point. His words are power. His breath is power. When something is God-breathed, it is life.

When the bones were properly assembled and even when the flesh was put on, when the spleen was positioned and the heart was nestled in and the lymphatic system was woven throughout and the brain was mounted in the skull, it was still not enough. The hair and the skin and eyes and fingerprints were all there. But Ezekiel knew it was not enough: "And I looked, and behold, sinews were on them, and flesh grew and skin covered them; but there was no breath in them" (Ezekiel 37:8). Even an armchair physician knows that you need blood and brain wave activity as well as air in order to live, but this vision was making a point. Without the breath of God, there is no life.

The last ingredient was the most significant. Just like at creation, it was only when the breath of God was involved that life began: "So I prophesied as He commanded me, and the breath came unto them, and they came to life and stood on their feet, an exceedingly great army" (Ezekiel 37:10). What was once a bone junkyard became a living army.

This was not a show. This was not presented for Ezekiel's entertainment. God was trying to teach him something – to teach us something. The breath of God would be essential to Ezekiel's assignment as God's prophet: "I will put My Spirit within you and you will come to life, and I will place you on your own land. Then you will know that I, the LORD, have spoken and done it" (Ezekiel 37:14). The breath of God (His Spirit) would provide life – the living authority that would prove God had indeed spoken.

THE SWORD

The breath of life carries spiritual significance. Just as we need air to survive physically, we need the Word of God (delivered through His breath, the Spirit) to survive spiritually.

The breath, the Spirit and the Word are all connected. In Revelation, God presented a startling image of Jesus through bold symbols:

"Out of His mouth came a sharp two-edged sword" (Revelation 1:16). Later in the same book, an identical image was used again: "From His mouth comes a sharp sword, so that with it He may strike down the nations" (19:15). Far from being a literal blade that slashes at physical enemies, this is the ultimate weapon for the ultimate enemy who attacks our very soul. [3]

This sword that appears again and again throughout Scripture is clearly associated with the Word: "For the Word of God is living and active and sharper than any two-edged sword, and piercing as far as the division of soul and spirit, of both joints and marrow, and able to judge the thoughts and intentions of the heart" (Hebrews 4:12). It is the weapon that determines the outcome of all spiritual conflict. [4] The sword, the Word, the breath of God: They are life for those who belong to the Creator and destruction for those who oppose Him.

QUESTIONS

1. How is the concept of breathing relevant to the concept of inspiration?

2. At what point did Adam become a living being?

3. Why is it important to know that God not only created us but also continues to sustain us?

4. What are some possible reasons why God designed us in such a way that we constantly need to breathe?

5. What are some of the key differences that God points out between Himself and idols?

6. What might be the significance behind idols not being able to breathe?

7. In the vision sent to Ezekiel, at what point did assembled bones come to life?

---

3 It is worth noting what Jesus said and did as He sent His apostles: "So Jesus said to them again, 'Peace be with you; as the Father has sent Me, I also send you.' And when He had said this, He breathed on them and said to them, 'Receive the Holy Spirit' " (John 20:21-22). Keeping in mind all that has been discussed in this chapter, it seems likely that Jesus' breath in this instance was an expression of life and authority as associated with the Spirit.

4 See also 2 Thessalonians 2:8.

8. What did God have Ezekiel do in order to bring the assembled bones to life?

9. How is this relevant to the modern Christian?

10. How is our relationship with the Word associated with our need to breathe?

Chapter 8

THE SPIRIT
OF GOD

They say history is written by the victors. This is meant to remind us that our records of the past are presented through the pens of those who won the battles. Since dead men tell no tales, it is up to the living men to describe what happened.

History is written by the victorious. But it is also written by the forgetful and the melodramatic. Everyone knows that even family stories retold through the years are subject to exaggeration, and they almost inevitably transform into fables with bonus materials that are undoubtably entertaining but not necessarily accurate.

We even find such glitches in the respectable pages of history. There are more than a few instances in which the history books have not been quite accurate. Paul Revere didn't ride for hundreds of miles shouting, "The British are coming!" He got about 11 miles before being detained by British soldiers. It was a man named Israel Bissell who rode for 4 days, covering about 350 miles and spreading the news of the impending British troops.

The Wright Brothers weren't the first men to fly. Orville and Wilbur did achieve a powered and manned flight in 1903. But a more accurate appraisal of the facts by modern aviators recognizes Gus Whitehead as the one who first achieved a powered and manned flight back in 1899.

The Declaration of Independence wasn't signed on July 4, 1776. The details of the document were discussed on that famous day, but the first signatures were penned on July 2.

Memories fade. Documents are lost. Propaganda corrupts. In the midst of such a faulty system of preserving the past, it would seem the Bible would be just as susceptible to such defects.

However, there is a very important reason the Bible was never in danger of being infiltrated by half-truths and fictions. The integrity of the Scriptures has always been in the hands of the Spirit of God. In fact, He has always been essential to the message.

DEEPLY INVOLVED

The Spirit has always been involved. Right from the very beginning, He was always an essential presence in the eternal purpose of God. At the time of creation, He was "moving over the surface of the waters" (Genesis 1:2). When Jesus was immersed "to fulfill all righteousness (Matthew 3:15), [1] the Spirit descended "as a dove" (v. 16). When Jesus returned to God, the Spirit instigated the power and authority of the church and led the apostles "into all the truth" (John 16:13). He even arrives on the scene of every baptism as a "gift" (Acts 2:38). The Holy Spirit has always been and always will be key to God's plan. From creation to re-creation, He is involved.

When the Holy Spirit was involved, things got done. The Spirit enabled Joseph to interpret Pharaoh's dream (Genesis 41:38). When Moses needed help in governing Israel, it was the Spirit who made 70 men qualified to take off some of the pressure (Numbers 11:17). Joshua was prepared to take Moses' place because he was "filled with the Spirit of wisdom" (Deuteronomy 34:9). In the book of Judges when it was time for the heroes of God to step up and take

---

1 Jesus is referred to as the "firstborn" of creation (Colossians 1:15). He made it clear that it was essential to be born of water and the Spirit (John 3:5). In the same part of the Bible, disciples were being baptized in a place called Aenon "because there was much water there" (v. 23). The vast numbers that responded to Peter's lesson on repentance strongly suggest that immersion was the defining moment of being "born" a second time just as Jesus was (Acts 2:41). Jesus Himself was of course sinless (Hebrews 4:15), but His immersion at the hands of John set the stage for the emphasis other Scriptures would place on the act of baptism (Acts 8:36; Romans 6:1-4; 1 Peter 3:21).

action, it was the Spirit who gave them the strength they needed to accomplish victory (Judges 3:10). [2]

THE SPIRIT AND THE PROPHET

One of the primary activities of the Spirit of God has been to deliver knowledge. Joseph had the inside information he needed to interpret Pharaoh's dream because the Spirit made him "discerning and wise" (Genesis 41:38-39). Saul sent messengers to take David by force, but the Spirit had the power to interfere with their plans, using them to prophesy: "Then Saul sent messengers to take David, but when they saw the company of the prophets prophesying, with Samuel standing and presiding over them, the Spirit of God came upon the messengers of Saul; and they also prophesied" (1 Samuel 19:20). Saul himself, despite his tendency to make decisions in opposition to God, was also given the Spirit of God so that he was able to prophesy: "Then the Spirit of the LORD will come upon you mightily, and you shall prophesy with them and be changed into another man" (10:6).

The Spirit is able to change a man into a prophet so that God's information is delivered regardless of the inclinations of the vessel. [3] It was the Spirit who made Jesus capable of being the Ultimate Teacher: "The Spirit of the LORD will rest on Him, the spirit of wisdom and understanding, the spirit of counsel and strength, the spirit of knowledge and the fear of the LORD" (Isaiah 11:2). When it came to delivering the Truth, the Spirit was involved.

So when it came time for God to establish the written form of His words, the Spirit of God was definitely involved. It was the Spirit who was deeply involved in securing the message through the apostles: "Do not worry about how or what you are to say; for it will be given you in that hour what you are to say. For it is not you who speak, but it is the Spirit of your Father who speaks in you" (Matthew 10:19-20).

---

2 Judges 6:34; 11:29; 13:25.

3 Because God is omniscient beyond time and space, even the future is not outside His awareness. That power in particular is impressive to those of us who are limited to only knowing the past and present. Therefore, a prophet knowing information about what has yet to happen stands out in our minds, but God did not just reveal knowledge about the future through His prophets. He also revealed knowledge about the past and present.

The apostles did not have to organize their opinions or make any outlines. It was not going to be a collection of personal insights on the matter. It was the Spirit speaking through them.

Because an apostle would be writing about some things he had actually witnessed, under normal circumstances, there was always the possibility something might slip his mind. Under normal circumstances, he might even remember it – but remember it wrong. Everybody knows that stories change if they are retold often enough. Family stories in particular get better and better, if not necessarily more accurate. However, the Spirit would make sure that details were not at the mercy of human memory: "But the Helper, the Holy Spirit, whom the Father will send in My name, He will teach you all things, and bring to your remembrance all that I said to you" (John 14:26). This would eliminate the possibility of contamination of the message through human flaws. The Spirit was the communicator.

SPIRITUALLY APPRAISED

The Spirit was not only instrumental in making sure the message was delivered, but He must also be presently involved in order to understand Scripture fully. He is the one who fully understands what God said:

> For to us God revealed them through the Spirit; for the Spirit searches all things, even the depths of God. For who among men knows the thoughts of a man except the spirit of the man which is in him? Even so the thoughts of God no one knows except the Spirit of God. (1 Corinthians 2:10-11)

In so many words, you can say that the Spirit can read God's mind. The Spirit has the job of moving information from the divine mind to the human mind. This is quite a leap downward, but it is possible:

> Now we have received, not the spirit of the world, but the Spirit who is from God, so that we may know the things freely given to us by God, which things we also speak, not in words taught by human wisdom, but in those taught by the Spirit, combining spiritual thoughts with spiritual words. (1 Corinthians 2:12-13)

This brings up an interesting aspect of the Word. In order for the Word to be fully received in the way it was intended, the Spirit must be active in the hearer. The Spirit is involved so that "we may know." The rest of the passage explains that it is possible not to know: "But a natural man does not accept the things of the Spirit of God, for they are foolishness to him; and he cannot understand them, because they are spiritually appraised" (1 Corinthians 2:14). Without the Spirit involved, the message is not completely delivered. Without the Spirit, the message cannot be truly received. He is essentially on both ends of the line of communication: On one end, He makes sure the message is accurately delivered, and on the other end, He makes sure it is accurately received.

Once we receive the Spirit at baptism, we are now linked to God in a way that other people are not. This is not a matter of religious snobbery. It is just the way this works. If you want God to have a clear line of communication with you, the Spirit must be involved.

This arrangement is a two-way avenue of communication. The Spirit delivered the Word of God, and He now affects us in such a way to keep our heads clear for things which are "spiritually appraised" (1 Corinthians 2:14). This is why a Christian has the "mind of Christ" (v. 16). Those who are not Christians do not have the mind of Christ. They may indeed do things that are Christlike, but anything "spiritually appraised" will be outside complete comprehension.

FROM MAN TO GOD

The Spirit is the one who establishes the necessary state of mind for comprehension, which allows for an amazing blessing: prayer. Prayer is probably one of the most neglected and underestimated blessings provided by God. Christians should be amazed that they have an audience with the King. The Designer and Creator of the universe is willing to hear the ones who have inevitably offended and denied Him through sin.

One of the best aspects of prayer is that there is no way for the one praying to be misunderstood. When a Christian prays, he or she is not limited to the semantic frailty of words:

> In the same way the Spirit also helps our weakness; for we
> do not know how to pray as we should, but the Spirit Himself
> intercedes for us with groanings too deep for words; and He
> who searches the hearts knows what the mind of the Spirit
> is, because He intercedes for the saints according to the will
> of God. (Romans 8:26-27)

The Spirit "intercedes for the saints," making sure nothing is lost in the journey between the physical realm and the heavenly one.

There is no chance of misrepresentation or misunderstanding. Otherwise, what a dangerous and fickle thing prayer would be. Anything we said could be misconstrued into a disaster. This would relegate prayer to nothing more than wishes – edgy requests brought to a genie who might deliver results with ironic twists.

The Spirit maintains the integrity of our message to God. At the point of transmission (our own minds), there is a high likelihood of flaws and confusion. Even we do not always know exactly what we are trying to say or even what we are trying to think. The Spirit is the safeguard against our mental shortcomings. Our less than perfect words do not stand in the way of our message. The communication is clear and perfect. Despite failure even at the point of origin, the system itself is flawless.

FROM GOD TO MAN

If the message from man to God is protected in such a powerful way, surely it is not unreasonable to expect the message from God to man is maintained in the same fashion. If anything, because the origin of transmission is perfect, the message is all the more likely to arrive as desired by the One who sent it. Granted, there is often failure on the receiving end, but delivery of the message is flawless.

God made it plain that even the Spirit would not make any adjustments to the message. It would be God's input and God's input alone:

> But when He, the Spirit of truth, comes, He will guide you
> into all the truth; for He will not speak on His own initiative,
> but whatever He hears, He will speak; and He will disclose
> to you what is to come. He will glorify Me, for He will take
> of Mine and will disclose it to you. (John 16:13-14)

God is the only One who has had any input on the matter. He has used the personalities and times of various writers. He has used the lens of their senses. Yet when it came to true inspiration, only the words He wanted were written down.

The Spirit is the Helper and Comforter. Part of His purpose is to make sure God and man communicate – in both directions. Just as our prayers arrive uncorrupted to God, God's own message has arrived uncorrupted to us.

QUESTIONS

1. What are some of the more familiar characteristics of the Spirit of God? the less familiar characteristics?

2. What are some of the ways the Spirit was specifically involved in delivering the truth in the Old Testament?

3. What particular facets of inspiration were/are overseen by the Spirit?

4. Why is it impossible for someone without the Spirit to interact fully with Scripture?

5. How is the Spirit involved in prayer?

6. What particular aspect of the Spirit concerning prayer might also be relevant to His involvement with inspiration?

7. Why is it safe to say that when it comes to Scripture, the point of origin is perfect?

8. Why is it safe to say that when it comes to Scripture, the method of transmission is perfect?

9. Why is it safe to say that when it comes to Scripture, if there is any failure to receive the truth, the receiving end is the most likely culprit?

Chapter 9

A HISTORY
OF HOLES

What started out as an organized march quickly degraded into a riot. In Ephesus, a man named Demetrius made a living fashioning silver shrines in honor of the goddess Artemis. Calling a meeting with his fellow craftsmen, Demetrius pointed out that Paul's teachings against idolatry were a clear threat to the market (Acts 19:24-27). As a unified group, they set out down the streets chanting, "Great is Artemis of the Ephesians!" (v. 28). They had a distinct and clear purpose.

As they moved through Ephesus, they collected others to the point that their numbers grew to an impressive extent. But something went wrong: "The city was filled with confusion, and they rushed with one accord into the theater" (Acts 19:29). Demetrius had set something big in motion. The only problem now was that the original purpose had become lost: "So then, some were shouting one thing and some another, for the assembly was in confusion and the majority did not know for what reason they had come together" (v. 32). Passion drowned out the purpose.

If there was ever a passage in the Bible that accurately describes the current state of the religious world today, this is the one. Some people are shouting one thing; some are shouting another. Everything is in confusion, and the majority don't even know why they're here.

Although the resurrection of Jesus set in motion a purpose with a specific direction, along the way things have, for the most part, gone wrong. The Truth was delivered, but the general result has been confusion.

TENDENCIES TOWARD CORRUPTION

The point of origin is flawless. The transmission is perfect as well. It's the reception that is questionable. It is up to us to make sure we are "accurately handling the word of truth" (2 Timothy 2:15). The delivery of God's Word is iffy only on the receiving end. This is where either clarity or confusion is born.

When the Word arrives at the gate of a man's mind, the message is pure. Nothing has been damaged or lost during the journey. But this is the location where the will of God confronts the will of man. Only those who have the Spirit received at baptism will be capable of accurately "discerning" the message. Even among these people, numerous obstacles can result in serious distortions. Unfortunately, the past is a strong indication that man will go to great lengths to alter the message. Approaching the Bible without the Holy Spirit, with a personal agenda, or with a tainted perspective can cloud the truth. By the time the Word runs any of these various gauntlets, much of the original message can be corrupted.

THREATS TO THE EARLY CHURCH

When the church was established, there were certainly contentions about the truth, but compared to the virtual chaos of religion today, the issues seem simple. Among Christians, the Word of God was the Word of God. Whether it was Jesus who spoke or His apostles or any other biblical writer, it was considered Truth: "They were continually devoting themselves to the apostles' teaching and to fellowship, to the breaking of bread and to prayer" (Acts 2:42). Within the church, the teaching of the apostles was the standard. If there was anyone among the Christians who stepped forward to try to refashion what had been taught, he would find himself facing unwavering authority.

This was the Truth, and it was treated as such. When an apostle wrote a letter to a congregation, it was standard procedure to make copies and circulate the letter among all the congregations. Thus, the book of Ephesians was not just for the Christians in Ephesus. It was the Word of God. This was for every Christian, then and now.

But it did not take long for uninspired reasoning to attempt to change the Truth: "But some of the sect of the Pharisees who had believed stood up, saying, 'It is necessary to circumcise them and to direct them to observe the Law of Moses' " (Acts 15:5). Failing to grasp the full significance of Jesus' fulfillment of the Old Law, these men were still trying to live inside the shadows of the Old Covenant instead of in the reality of the new.

The apostles addressed those who had been confronted with this issue: "We have heard that some of our number to whom we gave no instruction have disturbed you with their words, unsettling your souls" (Acts 15:24). The apostles went on to clear up the confusion through further instruction. Notice that the root of the problem was a lack of authorization. Efforts to bend the will of God to the will of man were identified as such and dismissed.

TWISTING SCRIPTURES

The history of religion reveals a progression of challenges to the Word. It is no surprise that man would make a virtual Babel of the message delivered by God. Large-scale attempts, such as the Nicene Creed (fourth century), were made to realign religious thinking. It was not the first or the last effort to settle doctrinal contention. But for the most part, the idea behind some of these gatherings was that the Word of God was the final authority on all spiritual matters.

Inevitably, men found themselves in disagreement concerning what the Bible taught. Adding to the confusion were ideas concerning how the Bible taught. Through the years, efforts were made to see the Bible in a "new" light, manipulating it or undermining it in such a way that ultimately served the will of man:

• In the second century, some of the Gnostics rejected the Pentateuch, three of the Gospels, and some of Paul's letters.

• In the third century, a man named Manichaeus announced that he was the Comforter as promised by Jesus. Manichaeus then began to "correct" certain books of the Bible and added a few of his own.

• In the fourth century, Aetius led the Anomaeans in teaching that some sections of the Bible should be discounted because certain parts were written when the writer was writing "as a man."

• In the fifth century, Theodore de Mopsuestia, who was head of a school in Antioch, claimed Job was merely a poem written by heathens.

• In the seventh century, Mohammed said the Bible was corrupted. He then began to add his own writings to it, presumably to correct it.

• In the 12th and 13th centuries, Jewish Talmudists set about establishing levels of inspiration. Various scriptures were relegated to this hierarchy. Others jumped on this idea, suggesting anywhere from three to 11 levels.

In one form or another, man would occasionally come up with a different system of interpretation, conveniently twisting Scripture to the current way of thinking. [1] This occurred on a grand scale in the 16th century, led by the sophisticated thinkers of that time. It was not that the world had lacked sophisticated thinkers before. But these thinkers in particular became less impressed with the Word and more impressed with their own minds. And as they felt more secure in their own thinking, they turned a doubting eye on Scripture. Learned men suggested that the Bible contained errors. In the 16th century, Socinus and Castellion taught that faulty memories kept the writers of the Bible from being infallible.

Their basic argument went back to the fact that the Bible was written by humans. They argued that because the writers were human, the information was subject to human error. Strangely enough, they seemed ignorant to the possibility of human error being found between their own ears. These "enlightened" intellects also began to argue that there were equal sources of authority other than the Word.

HIGHER CRITICISM
AND POSITIVE THEOLOGY

In the last part of the 18th century, a movement in Germany opposed the idea that the Bible was inspired, rejecting prophecies and suggesting

---

1 During the Medieval Age, one trend that surfaced was the practice of bibliomancy. The idea was to take a sacred book of some sort and open it to find a random message – in essence, a form of fortunetelling. People started applying this method to the Bible, treating it like a talisman suited for the occult.

that the miracles were simple allegories. The result was a movement known within religious circles as "higher criticism." [2]

A "lower criticism" (textual criticism) of the Bible had already been in use for quite some time. This involved deriving and deducing the original text from the current manuscripts available – a kind of security system that used copies and fragments in the original language for the sake of accuracy in translations.

"Higher criticism" was intended to be a greater exploration of the Bible. It set out to explore the influence of history on the biblical text, analyzing the repercussions of the authors' personalities and individual surroundings. In essence, "higher criticism" approached the book as if it had been composed by nothing more than human minds. The Bible was approached as if it were just any other book.

One of the primary aspects of "higher criticism" includes the idea that the writers of the Bible had great freedom as far as incorporating their perspective or even their own opinions. This assumption suggested that God was more of a ghost writer than the actual Author.

What followed was a free-for-all that resulted in numerous kinds of "higher criticism," each with its own idea of what interpretation should entail. Many intellectuals were now free to roam around the passages of Truth and lead their students in any direction they wanted. This is not to say that none of them were sincere in exploring these "untamed" ter ritories of doctrine, but with the absolute authority of God set aside, the Bible could be pillaged by even the most well-meaning religious scholar. Approaching the Bible as a man-made book provided countless loopholes, which could easily be used to serve the personal taste of every reader.

To make things even cloudier, "positive theology" also chimed in, pushing for the authority of the heart when it came to scriptural interpretation. So when it came time to choose between what the Word demanded and what emotion desired, many chose to follow their feelings. "Positive theology" encouraged people to let their hearts

---

2 The word "criticism" is not inherently negative, although today we do often have grounds for attaching darker connotations. However, the word "criticism" merely suggests an analysis. It is an examination to reveal the nature of a work. The results can be either positive or negative. Criticism is not automatically antagonistic to the object of its attention.

have the final say on matters. There was Scripture, but there were also emotion and experience. There was the doctrine of the Bible, and there was the doctrine of the heart.

Convinced they were living in a more informed and enlightened time, these men examined the Bible under a different lens. It was not a perspective that offered more clarity. It was a lens that curved the truth into any shape desired. Whereas "positive theology" put the heart in judgment over the Bible, "higher criticism" allowed the mind to sit in judgment over the Bible. Neither honored the Bible as the inspired Word of God.

The Bible itself requires that, when it comes to a relationship with God, both the mind and the heart be involved: "You shall love the Lord your God with all your heart, and with all your soul, and with all your mind" (Matthew 22:37). But when the fallible mind [3] and the foolish heart [4] are given precedent, truth will fall by the wayside.

CASTING DOUBTS

Armed with the world's idea of a sincere heart and an improved mind, the religious thinkers reached conclusions that cast doubt on Scripture. The Old Testament was reexamined and found to be doubtful as to its authenticity. Surely the events recorded were beyond belief. The educated and the enlightened concluded that the Old Testament contained myths. These "fables" served an admirable purpose, but they were nothing more than fiction designed to shape the morals of the reader.

At this point, many of the "educated" and the Bible were going their separate ways. Nothing in the Bible suggests that the events recorded in its pages are myths. Only an anti-supernatural bias suggested so. Jesus did not treat the Old Testament as such. As far as He was concerned, what was recorded in the Old Testament was nothing less than historical events recorded accurately.

Jesus often referred to events recorded in the Bible as if they were plain simple history. In order to explain the nature of His own Second Coming, He used the flood as an example: "For the coming of the Son

---

3 See also Proverbs 16:9; Romans 1:28; 8:6.
4 See also Psalm 81:12; Proverbs 6:18; 12:23.

of Man will be just like the days of Noah" (Matthew 24:37). He also
made a comparison between His own death and Jonah's experience
with the big fish: "Just as Jonah was three days and three nights in the
belly of the sea monster, so will the Son of Man be three days and three
nights in the heart of the earth" (12:40). Not once did Jesus indicate
that He was using a fable to make His point. He made reference to
these events in the offhand manner of someone who assumed that His
audience would take them for granted as being true.

A lawyer will not refer to fables if he wants to be taken seriously. It
is within the realm of possibility that he might allude to Pinocchio or
the three little pigs as amusing tangents, but not if he wants to shape
the thoughts of the jury on a significant level. Instead, a lawyer will
give precedence to relevant events of the past. A fictional arsenal would
not serve him as well as one of true events. Jesus was presenting the
most significant truths in existence. There is no evidence to suggest
that He used situations that never occurred.

Those who followed in the footsteps of Jesus treated the Old Testament
in the same fashion. Luke brought up the encounter Moses had with
the burning bush: "But that the dead are raised, even Moses showed,
in the passage about the burning bush, where he calls the Lord the
God of Abraham, and the God of Isaac, and the God of Jacob" (Luke
20:37). The reference is without qualification. Paul made reference to
the parting of the Red Sea in order to make a point about baptism: "For
I do not want you to be unaware, brethren, that our fathers were all
under the cloud and all passed through the sea; and all were baptized
into Moses in the cloud and in the sea" (1 Corinthians 10:1-2).

There is no indication that these writers were alluding to make-believe
events; rather, they treated them as factual, historical events. Regardless
of what the "educated" and emotional minds of the 16th century and
their intellectual descendants concluded, the Lord and His followers of
the first century considered the Old Testament events to be very true.

It is worth pointing out that the New Testament writers did not allude
to the low-impact stuff. The parting of the Red Sea was high-profile.
Sculpting an ocean would seem to be such a wild concept that referring
to it as part of your argument might cast doubt on your point. Calling
attention to the great flood as a vital precedent could come across as a

bad debate strategy. The immersion of the planet would seem a little over-the-top … unless it really happened. Paul and Peter and the others gestured to the events that were the most unlikely, the most miraculous (so to speak), the most defiant to the typical conditions of the natural world. But when reference was made to these events, no one blinked. In the minds of those who followed Jesus, there was no doubt that these things actually happened.

GOD'S WILL VERSUS MAN'S WILL

It is all a matter of what is being brought to the table. When faced with the Word of God – when the Bible is laid open – what can we offer as competition? The Bible is very clear that man's offerings to the debate are pitiful in comparison: " 'My thoughts are not your thoughts, nor are your ways My ways,' declares the LORD" (Isaiah 55:8). What God thinks and what man thinks will always be at odds unless the man humbles himself before his Creator. And when they are in conflict, it will always be God's perspective that is (or should be) considered the higher of the two: "For as the heavens are higher than the earth, so are My ways higher than your ways and My thoughts than your thoughts" (v. 9).

There is no contest. Man's ability to reason and his emotions are not even in the running. God expects the truth to shape our hearts and minds. Often with our minds and hearts, we try to shape the truth. This is where God's will and man's will go their separate ways.

The truth has been delivered. The source is perfect. The avenue of delivery is perfect. But man is fallible. The contrast and conflict of God's will and man's will is the point where we discover our true motivations. When faced with the often abrasive and offensive truth, what does a man do then? He attempts to use his mind against it. He attempts to change the truth to indulge his emotions. He appeals to what he considers as a higher court.

God's words are placed beneath the scrutiny of human thought and feeling. It has always been this way: "For you will no longer remember the oracle of the LORD, because every man's own word will become the oracle, and you have perverted the words of the living God, the LORD of hosts, our God" (Jeremiah 23:36). The sound of man's own mind and the roar of his own heart drown out the will of God. Each man becomes his own oracle and guide. A new pledge is implied: Man's will be done.

A man needs a heart that submits to God's Word. A man needs a mind that will submit as well. When faced with the truth, these must allow themselves to be transformed, fully ruled by the authority of our Creator. God's will be done. Period.

QUESTIONS

1. What are some of the most common modern perceptions about the nature of the Bible?

2. How does a failure to understand that the Old Covenant is obsolete tend to complicate current conclusions about Scripture?

3. What are some concepts throughout history that complicated man's approach to the Bible?

4. How does the promotion of human error among biblical writers shape people's perceptions of the Bible?

5. What are some of the dangers of "higher criticism"?

6. Why is the concept of authority so important when approaching the Bible?

7. How can our intellect interfere with an accurate approach to Scripture?

8. How can our emotions interfere with an accurate approach to Scripture?

9. Why is it misleading to consider some biblical events as fables or myths?

10. Why is an attitude of submission necessary when approaching the Word of God?

Chapter 10

THE RISE OF THE SOPHISTICATED READER

There is a common fable that most of us believe, that lives in the back of everyone's mind: We think we're sophisticated.

We are well into the 21st century. We are humanity, upgraded. We are the next best thing. Looking back on our dusty predecessors, we feel a certain amount of pity for them. They seem so simple and limited.

Without a doubt, we stand on an impressive height. Modern medicine is a welcome achievement, providing procedures that undeniably save lives. Our means of travel have allowed families to visit one another without letting such things as continents or oceans stand in the way. We are currently dismantling atoms and the crumbs of atoms, rewriting the book on the essential nature of matter. We are in the process of planning a manned mission to Mars. The average person carries enough gadgets that not long ago would have been possessed only by someone involved in espionage. [1]

---

1 Improvements are not only being made, they are being made faster and faster. Each generation is seeing more improvements during its lifetime than the generation before. We live in a world where everything is on the edge of becoming obsolete. Recently, we have become aware that certain aspects of our lives (including morality) are not keeping up with our technology. In some instances, technology can barely keep up with itself.

Standing in the glow of dazzling contraptions, the new and improved version of humanity hesitates when faced with the Bible – this book of antiquity. There is a strong sense that any relevance to the modern mind might have been worn away by the centuries. Presenting the Bible to the 21st-century mind seems a lot like trying to sell an eight-track tape to someone with an MP3 player.

THE ISSUE OF CULTURE

In honor of this gap between what we once were and what we are now, there is an effort to upgrade the Bible – to get it up to speed so that it can keep up with us as we hurtle into the ever-improving future. With good intentions, the Word is reconfigured and given a major overhaul. The idea is to make it more palatable for the sophisticated soul. Proud of our own minds, we stoop to adapt.

It is obvious that we live in a different culture than what was described in the Bible. This contrast is often the motivation to readjust doctrine. The assumption is that God delivered the Truth to the world but allowed the Truth to be shaped by the circumstances of that time period. The Word was delivered, but it conformed at least partially to the world. It follows then that because we are now in the midst of a different landscape of thought – a different time and place – it is necessary for the Word to conform once again.

The culture issue is fairly tricky when it comes to making contemporary adjustments. Researching the historical details of biblical times can indeed shed some light on Scripture. The setting was drastically different than the one we find ourselves in today. Even if you were to travel to the Middle East right now to attempt to achieve a greater sense of place, the stark contrast of time would still leave a distinctive gap – 21st-century Jerusalem is not first-century Jerusalem. One might feel a connection by visiting the Bible Lands, but the culture in which Jesus lived is irretrievable. The first-century church did not have the politics of petroleum or the ever-present shadow of nuclear weapons. They had the first-century equivalents of economic and militaristic concerns, but for the most part, antiquity's time and place are dead and gone.

It is worthwhile to try to reach across that gap as much as we can. Examining the culture of ancient history can be enlightening. Our modern ideas of planting seeds and catching fish are nothing like the ancient activities of the same name. Biblical concepts surrounding these activities do not come into full focus without some knowledge of "Bible times."

POPULAR DEMAND

To restrict the Word to the ancient culture does not work. Neither does trying to reshape it to fit our current one. However, in honor of our 21st-century minds, there are almost frantic efforts to make the Truth trendy. This approach often resorts to tactics that are ultimately a species of degradation. Driven by an apparent embarrassment of the "un-hipness" of the Bible, recent attempts to upgrade the Bible have resulted in a shallow parade of "Truth-ish" byproducts that have only a vague resemblance to the Word of God. A reverence for our sophistication has demanded that the Bible submit. Using the parameters of marketing techniques, the Bible is dismantled, repackaged and distributed as bumper stickers, T-shirts, concerts and virtually any means available. The world demands the Truth be given a makeover, and the pop-culture machine is ready to oblige.

The supremacy of popularity ends up shaping our relationship with God. This is nothing new. When faced with a decline in his own popularity, King Saul also made some compromises. When Samuel called him on it, Saul tried to explain his disobedience: "I saw that the people were scattering from me" (1 Samuel 13:11). He was losing numbers. So Saul made adjustments to God's commands. [2]

Today, concerned that the unadorned truth might offend or bore someone, decisions are made to adapt the words of God into something more palatable for the modern consumer. This seems especially true for religious activities aimed at youth. If any event is deemed "boring," you'll lose your audience. The deepest concern is not whether God is pleased but whether the young people are entertained. Just as the world of advertising is built on the latest criteria of "cool," so religion follows the whims of the youth.

---

2 King Jeroboam was also concerned about losing people. This is why he set up images in Bethel and Dan. These were not in honor of false gods. Jeroboam built these in honor of the true God, but they were still identified by God as idolatry (1 Kings 12:28-29).

USING CULTURE

Letting our current culture call the shots is a mistake, but any Christian would be wise to engage his surroundings to a certain extent. In fact, being familiar with the way the world thinks can ultimately provide opportunities for reaching the lost.

When Paul was in Athens, he was confronted by a circus of idols. Everywhere he looked, there was yet another affront to God. The Athenians seemed to be determined to worship every single solitary thing – except for the true Creator.

Paul studied this travesty and used it to reach the Athenians. Using the fantastical landscape of false teaching, he started with a basic observation: "I observe that you are very religious" (Acts 17:22). This was common ground. They were religious, and so was he. From there, he could start building the Truth.

In this case, Paul used cultural materials to construct a godly message. His lesson was built on the idols of Athens, but his message did not succumb to the games of idolatry itself. He did not bring the Truth down into the fields of false gods. He strolled through there briefly, but only to lead the people as quickly as possible away from that circus. As with all Christians, he was in the world but not of the world.

THE INFLUENCE OF CULTURE

One of the greatest risks of the culture issue is that it can provide a handy loophole for just about any idea, even for those sporting exceptionally worldly concepts. Someone with practically no knowledge of Scripture can play the culture card to try to trump doctrine. It is easy to set aside just about any command of God by attempting to discount His words as irrelevancies deeply entangled in culture.

This line of thinking seems to suggest that God allowed culture to shape the Truth. Just as some suggest God allowed human thinking to determine the dimensions of His Word, others in a similar fashion suggest He allowed human culture to do the same.

This concept falters in light of the fact that some of the Bible is rooted in pre-cultural circumstances. When Jesus taught God's will concerning marriage, He alluded to the Garden of Eden (Matthew 19:4-9). To suggest that this command was influenced by culture is quite a reach.

Even if an anthropologist loosened up the definition of "culture" in order to apply it to Adam and Eve, he would then be hard-pressed to try to prove the circumstances had any sway over God's commands in that time and place. God created the circumstances.

When it came time to have His Word written down, God not only chose the right men; He also chose the right time and place. The ancient Middle East served that purpose. But nothing in this choice suggests we can now trim away the things that offend our own time and place. The Word of God arrived like Jesus did – unfazed by the surroundings. Jesus did not pull any punches because it might be out of line with current thinking. He did not "lighten up" to make His lessons more user-friendly.

Even His enemies knew this: "And they sent their disciples to Him, along with the Herodians, saying, 'Teacher, we know that You are truthful and teach the way of God in truth, and defer to no one; for You are not partial to any' " (Matthew 22:16). When it came time for Jesus to speak up, when it came time for anything God had to say through inspiration, there was no submission to the surroundings. [3] This is part of the reason they ended up killing Him. The message did not adapt to the ones hearing it. It was and always has been the other way around. When the Word arrives, everything else must submit.

DANGEROUS REINTERPRETATIONS

When the Word and the world are at odds, sudden reevaluations spring up. Faced with Scripture that is too abrasive to the modern mind, many turn to abrupt reinterpretations of relevant passages. It seems some-what suspicious that just when it happens to be popular, we discover something that the Bible actually meant to say about male leadership or homosexuality. The timing is highly suspect. It effectively allows us to control the Word instead of the other way around.

---

3 Jesus' parables included common and familiar images from the current culture, but they were never designed to lighten up the truth. In fact, the parables were designed to separate the men from the boys, so to speak (Matthew 13:13-16). The parables set apart those who were really looking for answers.

There are numerous ways to keep the Bible on a short leash. The concept of a "core gospel" has also served this purpose. The basic concept suggests there is a central truth or theme in the Bible and that the rest is a sort of peripheral truth. This implies that other parts of the Bible are "non-essential." This parallels the same thinking that holds up Jesus' red letters as more significant than the rest of Scripture. Something written by Paul might be set aside because it is not part of the "core."

If there really is a "core," to what point do we pare things down? If the Scripture can by whittled down to essentials, when do we stop? Someone once facetiously suggested that it might be eerily appropriate to reduce it all down to "Jesus wept."

INTELLECTUAL OBSTACLES

Unfortunately, this arrogant dissection often thrives best in the halls of education. One of the greatest blessings God ever provided was the ability to increase our knowledge. Many, many people fall far short of their potential, squandering their capabilities and drowning in mindless distractions. Education is the means by which a person can really make his or her talents shine. But the pursuit of knowledge itself can ruin someone's potential just as effectively as the lack of it. Education itself is not to blame, but it can help promote the illusion of sophistication.

God warns us against becoming too enthralled with our own brains: "For as the heavens are higher than the earth, so are My ways higher than your ways and My thoughts than your thoughts" (Isaiah 55:9). Just because certain ones have extra pieces of the alphabet following their name does not disqualify them from plain old basic foolishness. Numerous degrees do not a wise man make.

Although the constantly changing stream of fads is sweeping away reverence for the Truth, it often seems that man's infatuation with his own mind is what ultimately powers this coup. Just as the 18th century produced scholarly thinkers who attempted to promote and publish their doubts concerning the reliability of Scripture, we have our own modern species of the same.

It is easy to fall into this trap. There are difficult passages in the Bible, which require much effort and thought and study. A person with "smarts" might indeed grasp a concept that eludes someone else. This makes it easy to believe greater truths are buried away that can be dug up only by an intellectual. Surrounded by lexicons and concordances, this person might very well be deceived into thinking he has access to truths that others do not.

This can be dangerous. It can smack of gnosticism. The impressive intellect can actually end up being an obstacle. In the midst of being very brilliant, one can forget the possibility that one might be very wrong.

THE DANGER OF HERMENEUTICS

One tool that has the potential for causing much damage is hermeneutics or the science of interpretation. There is, of course, a great benefit to systemizing an approach to Bible study. Certain guidelines serve us well when trying to understand Scripture. You cannot just barrel into passages without using your head.

The problem is that hermeneutics can inadvertently suggest that a scientific approach alone is suitable for understanding Scripture – that if we establish some kind of flow chart or a procession of bullet points, we can methodically derive the Truth. Investing in the scientific mindset, we then feel confident in our conclusions.

Hermeneutics was developed during the Protestant Reformation to support the idea that everyone should have access to Scripture. Because the Bible was such a significant book and because it was sometimes difficult to understand, an effort was made to come up with a system to get to the truth of the text. So people began to write about how to interpret the Bible.

Then came constitutional democracies. Because people considered this new approach to be both important and sometimes difficult to understand, the concept of hermeneutics was then applied to the study of law. What had originally been designed to interpret Scripture was now applied to man-made laws. Hermeneutics was used to define what was constitutional and was not.

Eventually, hermeneutics found its way into literature. Unfortunately, during the 18th century, some of the literature began to become very impressed with itself. Romanticism promoted the idea that the author was, in a sense, divine. Writing became more about drawing attention to the genius of the author. It was not long before literature was thought of as a kind of "secular scripture" in which the meaning was thought to be extremely significant and extremely difficult to understand. For many people, poetry became their "scripture."

Over the years, hermeneutics has not only changed how we see literature, but literature has also changed how we see hermeneutics. It is not uncommon during a literature course to be confronted with a dizzying arsenal of various styles of interpretation. There is the concept of the "hermeneutic circle," which suggests that the reader inevitably becomes part of the text's meaning. This psychoanalytic approach dwells on potential symbolism anchored in the subconscious. Deconstruction teaches that ultimately the text has no meaning at all.

THE NATURAL MAN

If this kind of sophistry finds its way into the mind of someone studying the Bible, it is no wonder we end up with a great deal of confusion. Scholars are not the enemy. Only a fool would relish ignorance. However, some fairly foolish ideas are walking the halls of higher education. Anyone would do well to be somewhat wary of what some intellectuals bring to the table.

There is a key flaw in trying to approach the Bible armed solely with academic criteria: "But a natural man does not accept the things of the Spirit of God, for they are foolishness to him; and he cannot understand them, because they are spiritually appraised" (1 Corinthians 2:14). The Word of God is "spiritually appraised," not intellectually analyzed. As mentioned before, only those who have the Holy Spirit can accurately receive what is spiritually appraised. Even the most dazzling intellect is going to come up against a brick wall if the reader is delving into the Word without the Holy Spirit. A man might indeed spend years learning Scripture and even be able to line up all the facts. But to grasp the truth of the Word, the Spirit must be involved.

Anyone who does not belong to God is going to be incapable of completely incorporating the Truth: "The mind set on the flesh is hostile toward God; for it does not subject itself to the law of God, for it is not even able to do so" (Romans 8:7). Anyone who does not belong to God will be in conflict with the Author. This will not be conducive to reaching accurate conclusions concerning His Word. Regardless of how sophisticated and educated and graduated a man might be, he is no match for a Christian when it comes to understanding the Bible.

English literature majors often study critical theory to learn different ways to analyze various works methodically. A great deal of it is useful for not only understanding difficult concepts but also for simply improving the student's ability to write and think clearly. Sometimes, however, proponents of critical theory seem to suggest that, ultimately, every book must submit to the intellect of the one who opens it.

One trend within these circles is worthy of note. When it comes to literary interpretation, you will hear the word "writer" more often than the word "author." The first has less substance than the second. The term "author" is too closely associated with the word "authority" for modern tastes. In this manner, the writer becomes secondary to the reader. Books are analyzed and diagnosed with the belief that the reader will ultimately determine what the book has to say. In at least one instance, when the reader presented his interpretation of a book to the author himself, the exchange went something like this:

Reader: "You meant such-and-such when you wrote your book."

Author: "No. That's not what I meant at all."

Reader: "Actually, you did. You meant such-and-such subconsciously."

With this kind of logic running loose, it is no wonder that we end up involved in discussions that would be right at home in *Alice In Wonderland*. Apply this kind of foolery to Bible study, and the sublime quickly becomes ridiculous.

OUR UNCHANGED NATURE

Convinced we are sophisticated, we have a tendency to look down on even the Word of God. Still, some things remain that might keep us humble. Recent analysis of the modern thinker indicates that our technology is producing cloudy-headed pawns rather than the expected race of geniuses. On top of that, we still cannot predict the weather. You may have also noticed that despite our array of medical champions, we are all still dying.

If these things are not enough to keep us humble, greater humiliations may be in store. God gives grace to the humble, but He opposes the proud (1 Peter 5:5). You do not have to develop a doomsday mentality to make such predictions.

Most of all, we need to know one thing in particular: Nothing has changed. At the risk of bursting our 21st-century bubble, it must be pointed out that we have not improved at all. If anything, our technology often provides the means merely to make mistakes twice as fast with greater consequences.

The Bible is and always will be acutely relevant for one important reason. Man has not changed – not even a little bit. There is no significant difference between you and, say, Elijah: "Elijah was a man with a nature like ours" (James 5:17). Having keys in your pocket and a phone in your ear does not make you the über-human. You haven't outrun the Bible. Just like the next guy, you are the same spiritually battered, pitiful soul that defines all humanity. The good news is that this makes you a perfect candidate for heaven through the blood of Jesus. When we get to heaven, we will have a much more accurate perspective. Then we'll talk sophistication.

QUESTIONS

1. What is it about modern man that makes him feel sophisticated?

2. Why is it important to approach the issue of culture and Scripture with some caution?

3. How did Jesus indicate He was not letting the culture of His time shape the message?

4. Why is it unwise to attempt to adapt the Word in order to make it more palatable to cultural trends?

5. How has a marketing mentality affected the religious world?

6. Why is it important to be cautious of terms such as "essential" and "non-essential"?

7. What are some of the advantages/disadvantages of higher education?

8. How can hermeneutics be a help in approaching the Bible? How can it be a hindrance?

9. Why will the Bible always be relevant?

Chapter 11

THE MAN
AND THE PLAN

T here is an old story often told from the pulpit involving a little boy who was too scared to go to sleep. When his mother found him awake long after bedtime, she sat with him, trying to comfort him. After a few moments, she got up and started to leave again, assuring her son there was no reason to be afraid because God was with him.

"Yeah," her son commented with some hesitation, "but I need someone with skin on him."

Inadvertently, this little boy gave a somewhat crude description of Jesus, who was nothing less than God in the flesh. All of God's plans were manifested in Jesus. God had been communicating to the world in order to establish His plan for salvation. Although the messages varied in content and were delivered in numerous ways, the heart of each message was the same. God would send His Son to save the world. Every conversation between God and man and every event recorded – all point to the arrival of Jesus.

THE LAST MESSAGE

Although God used many forms of communication, Jesus would have the final word: "God after He spoke long ago to the fathers in the prophets in many portions and in many ways, in these last days has spoken to us in His Son, whom He appointed heir of all things, through whom also He made the world" (Hebrews 1:1-2). Jesus and those who received His inspired revelations would close out everything God had to say to the world.

There would be nothing vague about this last message. There would be nothing unclear when it came to Jesus. Everything about God was brought into focus through Him: "And He is the radiance of His glory and the exact representation of His nature" (Hebrews 1:3). The Bible has no static – just a straightforward message embodied in Jesus. Any failure to comprehend would be a measure of the one who approached Him.

THE HUMANITY AND DIVINITY OF JESUS

When Jesus set foot on the earth, He was the culmination of all the words and pages that had come before. Every prophet was pointing to what Jesus would have to say. Distraught about Jesus and His message, many believed that He had come to erase or rebel against what had been sent by God before. But Jesus made it clear that what had been sent before was all a prelude to Himself: "Do not think I came to abolish the Law or the Prophets; I did not come to abolish but to fulfill" (Matthew 5:17). Jesus arrived to put the final touches on God's eternal plan: "These are My words which I spoke to you while I was still with you, that all things which are written about Me in the Law of Moses and the Prophets and the Psalms must be fulfilled" (Luke 24:44). What God began under the Old Covenant, Jesus would complete. The shadows of the old would be reality in the new. [1]

The tabernacle was just such a shadow. It was not merely a place of worship. It was a structure designed to contain the presence of God even while He was in the midst of His people. It was somewhat similar to having a highly unstable nuclear reactor in a residential area. Great precautions were necessary, and all life was shaped around the ever-present danger that it represented. No enemy of Israel could withstand such a

---

1 Hebrews extensively develops the idea of the Old Covenant being the shadow (or copy) and the New Covenant being the reality (Hebrews 8:5; 9:24; 10:1). This is in connection with the types and antitypes used throughout the Bible (Romans 5:14; Hebrews 11:19).

presence, but neither could any Israelite himself if the tabernacle was treated as anything less than holy. Enemies died, but so did Israelites. But this was not a permanent arrangement. The tabernacle and all the activities involved with it were designed to point to the ultimate tabernacle. Just as the tabernacle was a physical representation of God among the people, Jesus would be the same: "And the Word became flesh, and dwelt among us, and we saw His glory, glory as of the only begotten from the Father, full of grace and truth" (John 1:14). In this passage, the term "dwelt" actually comes from the word "tabernacle." The passage literally reads, "the Word became flesh and tabernacled among us."

He was not just the tabernacle fulfilled, He was the ultimate high priest. Only the high priest was allowed under precarious circumstances to enter the Most Holy Place. But this room was only a shadow of heaven. And only Jesus could qualify as the ultimate High Priest actually allowed to enter this realm.

He was the perfect combination of divinity and humanity. There were those – and still are – who question the divine nature of Jesus. It is a tired issue that no less defines an antichrist. [2] The Bible claims that Jesus was the human version of God. Neither aspect canceled out the other. He was a perfect fusion of both natures.

Doubts usually focus on His humanity. Because He was human, it is argued that He was in some small way humanly flawed. However, Scripture makes it clear that He was human in all ways, but He was also perfect in all ways: "For we do not have a high priest who cannot sympathize with our weaknesses, but One who has been tempted in all things as we are, yet without sin" (Hebrews 4:15). This is deeply significant, for only a perfect sacrifice would have been enough not just to cover sin but to remove it completely.

---

2 To avoid a topic that would be a tangent in this case, here are some quick thoughts about the antichrist. Although the religious world pushes for a solitary foe with fantastical accessories, the antichrist is much more dangerous than a Hollywood fiend who scowls from some future throne or the Oval Office. The book of 1 John gives a plain and straightforward definition (1 John 2:22). Also, take notice that we are dealing in plural, not singular (v. 18). To be an antichrist, you simply have to deny that Jesus is God. With that definition, we have plenty to go around. You do not have to summon fire or infiltrate congress to destroy souls. All you have to do is promote the lie that Jesus is not God.

THE HUMANITY AND DIVINITY OF THE BIBLE

The tabernacle came and went. Jesus came and went. Yet we are still left with a physical representation of God that lives among us just as Jesus did: the Word of God. This is why Jesus and the Word are used interchangeably. He was the voice, the logos, the breath of God. He was how the "Word became flesh" (John 1:14). The Word is one of the many names of Jesus used to explain His purpose and nature. "His name is called the Word of God" (Revelation 19:13). The Word and Jesus are closely associated. He is called "the Word of Life" (1 John 1:1). If you are dealing with Jesus, you are dealing with the Word and vice versa.

As the manifestation of God, Jesus took on the "likeness of men" (Philippians 2:7). He took on "flesh and blood," the materials that would be used by God to communicate with man (Hebrews 2:14). Just as the tabernacle was made of cloth and gold, Jesus was made of flesh and bone. The cloth and gold, the flesh and bone were physical tools used to serve a spiritual purpose.

This is also true of the Bible. The Bible is the breath of God, the voice of God, and the physical representation of His nature just as Jesus was. The metaphor of Jesus as the Word means something. They were used interchangeably for a reason.

The Bible is also a fusion of divinity and humanity. Just as Jesus was completely God and completely human, so is the Bible. If the Bible was anything less than this, God would not have set His Son side-by-side with His Book as He did. Whatever Jesus could have accomplished by remaining here, the Word can accomplish instead. If not, then God left us with a lesser chance of finding our own salvation. We have the same chance of reaching heaven as anyone who ever walked with the physical flesh and blood Jesus. We have the same chance because we are "walking" with the equivalent.

PARALLEL TACTICS

As almost a reversed form of honor, the same disrespect and doubt that circled Jesus also circles the Word. Just as there were efforts to reduce the Son of God to just another man from Nazareth, there are parallel efforts today to reduce the Word to just another book.

Those who were opposed to what Jesus had to say misrepresented Him. Modern opponents do the same to the Word. The opponents of Jesus listened to Him until He started telling them things they did not want to hear. Modern opponents do the same to the Word. Faced with the undeniable divinity of Jesus, His opponents tried to destroy Him. Modern opponents do the same to the Word.

Many religious people would never dream of questioning the deity of Jesus. Yet many question the divinity of the book that God holds up next to Jesus as His equal. The Word became flesh and dwelt among them. The Word is now paper and dwells among us. Just as Jesus was the exact representation of God, so is the Word.

THE HUMANITY AND DIVINITY OF THE CHURCH

Yet another presence that is both divine and human might at first seem to be an exception to the rule. The church is composed of godly people, and no one is blind enough to suggest that any congregation is free of imperfections. In fact, it might be the best place to find them.

It is a cold realization the day you find yourself being treated better by those out in the world than by your brothers and sisters in the church. Just about any example of sin can be found among the called-out. Only the blindest of all would be blind enough not to realize he himself brings his own contributions to such imperfections.

Jesus left, and in His place, He left the church. He remains the head of the church, but it is the flesh and blood organism that has been assigned the monumental task of taking His place. Whereas one Man once walked the earth teaching the truth and saving souls, now numerous men and women do the same. But this body often seems a stumbling monstrosity compared to the ultimate Man that was here before. He did not make any mistakes. As members of the church, we are wallowing in them.

So how is this not an example of an imperfect fusion of deity and humanity?

Don't miss it: The church is perfect. That was always the plan. Jesus lived in such a way as to "present to Himself the church in all her glory, having no spot or wrinkle or any such thing; but that she would be holy and blameless" (Ephesians 5:27). Regardless of the sin that can be found in any Christian's life, the forgiveness provided through the blood of Jesus results in a perfected body of Christians. Knowing full well that He would be leaving flawed men in charge, Jesus established the means by which the imperfect could be made perfect: "If we walk in the Light as He Himself is in the Light, we have fellowship with one another, and the blood of Jesus His Son cleanses us from all sin" (1 John 1:7). The Light of the Word constantly reshapes a Christian so that he or she might resist becoming like the world and become more like Jesus: "And do not be conformed to this world, but be transformed by the renewing of your mind, so that you may prove what the will of God is, that which is good and acceptable and perfect" (Romans 12:2). The church is made clean "by the washing of water with the word" (Ephesians 5:26). Despite shortcomings, if Christians continue to strive toward obedience, the church is constantly perfected. And this is accomplished by what is perfect: the Word.

This assignment was given even before the world was created: "He chose us in Him before the foundation of the world, that we would be holy and blameless before Him" (Ephesians 1:4). Faced with our imperfections, only Jesus can make us so. But it takes a constant striving on our part. "And this I pray, that your love may abound still more and more in real knowledge and discernment, so that you may approve the things that are excellent, in order to be sincere and blameless until the day of Christ" (Philippians 1:9-10). This blamelessness comes through the blood of Christ, and we sustain our grip on it by turning to real knowledge and discernment. Only the Word can provide this. The church has no authority to bypass or override anything that Scripture says.

Yet the church itself is a union of divinity and humanity. And although it often falters, it is perfectly maintained by the perfect Word. So the exception proves the rule.

Jesus as a human being was the perfect representative of God. He accomplished everything He was sent to do. The Word also has an assignment, and it will also accomplish everything it was sent to do. As the imperfect, we are perfected by the blood of Jesus. We then diligently seek the discernment that comes from the Word to strive toward a perfection we will never achieve. Only a perfect book could serve such a purpose of saving us from being conformed to the world. Only a perfect book can reshape us to be more and more suitable for the perfection of heaven.

QUESTIONS

1. What are some of the methods God has used to communicate with man over the years?

2. Compared to all the other methods of communication, why is it that God communicating through His Son is so drastically different?

3. What was the relationship between Jesus and the Old Covenant?

4. What is the connection between the tabernacle and Jesus?

5. Why is it so vital that Jesus was completely human?

6. Why is it so vital that Jesus was completely God?

7. How is the Word of God like Jesus? How is the Word of God like the tabernacle?

8. How is questioning the divinity of the Word similar to questioning the divinity of Jesus?

9. How is the church also a combination of humanity and divinity?

10. How is the Word an essential factor in the nature of the church?

Chapter 12

TACTICS
OF THE ENEMY

W e have an enemy. All other villains are pale imitations of him. His very name means "adversary." It would be nearly impossible to exaggerate the animosity that motivates his every move. His malevolence toward God is demonstrated toward us. Because he cannot harm God Himself, he harms those whom God loves. But Satan is not a suave king of the underworld. He is a mortally wounded animal desperate to lash out and take as many down with him as possible.

Strangely enough, he is often portrayed in humorous terms. Many imagine him to be a lounging annoyance tampering with our days like a malevolent wizard. Others see him only as a laughable character surrounded by cartoon flames – setting up a punch line.

We have an enemy, and one of the best ways to play into his hands is to underestimate him.

God gave us plenty of warning concerning our enemy: "Be of sober spirit, be on the alert. Your adversary, the devil, prowls around like a roaring lion, seeking someone to devour" (1 Peter 5:8). We have no reason to be caught off guard: "We are not ignorant of his schemes" (2 Corinthians 2:11). How foolish to choose ignorance when it comes to the original and ultimate enemy.

REMOVING THE WORD

Despite common belief, Satan is not the opposite of God. He is definitely in direct opposition, but he is no match for the Creator. There is no yin-yang balance in this equation. In this conflict, Satan has not got a chance. But because God will not force anyone to love Him and because He will allow the free choice of rejecting Him, God will allow anyone to succumb willingly to our adversary.

If we have a firm grasp of who is trying to ruin us, we will consider the strong likelihood that one of his primary targets will be the Word. His goal is to destroy us. Certainly this plan would entail attacking God's Word. If he is able to destroy the Word, then he has destroyed us.

The Bible is our means of survival. It is our daily bread. It is the very breath of life that sustains our souls. Take out this source and we are done for.

In A.D. 300, the emperor Diocletian determined to wipe out Christianity. He was so confident in the success of this endeavor he had a "column of triumph" built to commemorate the demise of all Christians. Knowing that the Bible was key to the survival of the movement, he intentionally inflated the price of Scripture. During his reign, a copy of the New Testament would have cost the equivalent of $512 in modern U.S. currency. A complete copy of the Bible went for the equivalent of $2,800. Diocletian was the greatest power on earth, and he used every facet of his power to erase the Word of God.

• During the 1200s, Gregory IX of Spain ordered the people bring in their Bibles to be burned.

• In the 1300s, the Bible was banned.

• Ferdinand and Isabella (the patrons of Columbus) banned the Bible in the 1400s.

• During the 1500s, the pope urged bishops to prevent laymen from reading the Bible.

To a certain extent, our enemy did some damage. There were times when people lived in ignorance. Access to the Scripture was limited. But the Word survived. For all of the adversary's efforts, the Word remained intact. It has become quite clear (maybe even to our enemy) that the Word of God will always survive, just as it promises: "But the Word of the Lord endures forever" (1 Peter 1:25). The inspired words of God are here to stay.

CORRUPTING OUR PERSPECTIVE

But our enemy has other options. If he cannot destroy the Word itself, he can destroy an accurate perspective of it. If Satan cannot take it from us, he can distort our view of it, essentially destroying it, one individual at a time.

Interestingly enough, one of Satan's best tools for this strategy and for many of his schemes is religion itself. During one of his efforts to ruin Jesus, Satan quoted Psalm 91, using Scripture of all things as a weapon against the Son of God (Matthew 4:6). Our enemy may not be able to remove the Word of God, but he can certainly try to corrupt it.

One method that has proven very effective for him in religious circles has been the modern use of the term "Pharisee." If the Bible is the perfectly inspired Word of God, then a Christian is clearly going to be fully dedicated to doing exactly what it teaches. This kind of devotion is often undermined by throwing around the accusation of "Pharisee," which is often accompanied by the word "legalism." This is meant to be a rebuke based on the first-century opponents of Jesus who several times served as examples for those who were religiously off-track.

In modern religious conversations, the Pharisee is thought to be a person so obsessed with following God's Word that he steps all over souls to get it done. Justifying unkindness and even cruelty in the name of doctrine, the Pharisee tramples his way to self-righteousness. This is true – to a point.

THE TRUE PHARISEE

The Pharisees in Jesus' day were not really devoted to God's Word. They were devoted to their ideas based on God's Word. There is a big difference here. Jesus did not routinely reprimand the Pharisees because they were too adamant about obeying God's Word. Take a step back, and anyone can see that this would be a laughable accusation coming from the One who was "obedient to the point of death" (Philippians 2:8). The problem had nothing to do with obeying God's commands.

The problem was that they were twisting the commands of God to fit man's agenda: "Why do you yourselves transgress the commandment of God for the sake of your tradition?" (Matthew 15:3). [1] Jesus ripped away their righteous veneer and revealed them for what they were. They just seemed as if they were obeying God. But being a Pharisee was not about obeying God:

> He said to them, "Rightly did Isaiah prophesy of you hypocrites, as it is written, 'This people honors Me with their lips, but their heart is far away from Me. But in vain do they worship Me, teaching as doctrines the precepts of men.' Neglecting the commandment of God, you hold to the tradition of men." He was also saying to them, "You are experts at setting aside the commandment of God in order to keep your tradition." (Mark 7:6-9) [2]

They were not loyal to the Sabbath. They were loyal to their idea of the Sabbath as dictated by uninspired, religious, popular thinking. A passing glance of a Pharisee looked a lot like a man of God. But he was actually a man of man.

Jesus had to get after Peter for similar reasons. When Jesus explained His plan involving His death and resurrection, Peter opposed it. He was apparently motivated by concern for Jesus, but he was way off. Jesus explained the reason for Peter's faulty reasoning: "You are a stumbling block to Me; for you are not setting your mind on God's interests, but man's" (Matthew 16:23). Although Peter was determined and although he was genuine, he was misguided because he was basing his "theology" on man's interests.

Later, Paul made it a point to fall into the same trap: "For am I now seeking the favor of men, or of God? Or am I striving to please men? If I were still trying to please men, I would not be a bond-servant of Christ"

---

1 The traditions of men were condemned, not the traditions of God. There have been times in the past when "witch hunts" for anything that might be tradition have been instigated in the name of fighting legalism. Jesus never condemned the traditions of the Word. It was always about misguided loyalty to traditions as established by the current worldly trends and thinking.

2 See also Matthew 23:23; Mark 7:13; Luke 11:42; John 12:43.

(Galatians 1:10). [3] Striving to follow the commands of Scripture adamantly does not make one a Pharisee. A Pharisee fashions a "truth-ish" philosophy based on his own ideas or the ideas of the men who went before him. It is plain and simple self-indulgence (Matthew 23:25). At the risk of sounding trite, we could say that a Pharisee's theology is actually "me-ology." [4]

If someone is deeply devoted to following the Word, call him a zealot. Call him a fanatic. But do not call him a legalistic Pharisee. The ones who are riding the trends of pop-religion are more suitable candidates.

A misuse of the term Pharisee is a very effective tool for Satan. It is a term that can cast doubt on anyone determined to trust God's Word. It suggests that it is a shortcoming to take the Bible seriously.

THE FIRST ATTACK

Our enemy's first attack on mankind was this very strategy. After creation was up and running, God communicated directly with its sole occupant. He communicated with the only man that currently existed. One God, one earth, one man – about as simple an arrangement as possible. He explained to Adam His will. He made it very clear: No one was to eat from the tree of the knowledge of good and evil. The source of the message was perfect. The delivery was perfect. The problem was, as always, in the reception.

Add one woman. Still, the connection with God is intact. The Truth is still crystal clear.

Add one enemy – an enemy who knows where to strike: on the receiving end.

Satan approached the woman: "Now the serpent was more crafty than any beast of the field which the LORD God had made. And he said to the woman, 'Indeed, has God said … ?' " (Genesis 3:1). Here it is: A handful of words, but a lethal tactic. God spoke, then Satan approached those on the receiving end and began the deconstruction of the Garden of Eden with a few words. "Has God said … ?" is the

---

3 This kind of corruption can be found today in both liberal and conservative camps. Each Christian should examine and reexamine his beliefs to make sure his doctrine is not built only on sound bites, catchy phrases and family favorites that he picked up along the way.

4 See also 1 Thessalonians 2:4.

essence of the problem. As one preacher suggested, "Everything was fine until someone opened it up for discussion."

We have a choice. Faced with the Bible, we either take it as the inspired Word of God, ready to let it shape our will, or we can ask "Has God said … ?" and use our will to attempt to shape the Word of God.

If the Bible is kind of the truth – if the Bible is mostly God's Word – it is no wonder that people in general are not motivated to read it, let alone devote themselves to it. This might be the most damaging thing of all. The enemy has convinced many of us only to sort of believe in the Word of God.

BANNING THE BIBLE

We are fortunate to live in a country that allows us to read the Bible. For now, there is no Diocletian or Gregory IX to step in and attempt to destroy the Bible or those who read it. In most cases, anyone can pick up a Bible at any time and read it. But no one does.

Maybe we should ban the Bible.

One of the best ways to make sure that a book is read is to ban it. Something inside us becomes motivated if there are blatant attempts to oppress our thinking or our choices. Many of the books and movies that have been ostracized in the past would have never had the attention they gained if no one had pointed them out as worthy of rejection. In urging people to ignore it, they only drew attention to it.

So maybe we should ban the Bible. If someone were to tell people they could not read the Bible, maybe people actually would. Apparently, almost no one is reading it right now. It is hard to say why. Either they do not believe it is the Word of God, or they believe it is only sort of the Word of God.

We read books about the Bible. We listen to people talk about the Bible. We own a Bible and might even carry it around. We will swear on the Bible and possibly even rise up and bear arms to protect our right to have one, but we certainly will not read it.

Which is worse: a nation banning the Bible or an individual? We have a country literally filled with Scripture. Yet on the individual level, the banishment is in place. This is no exaggeration. If we have not whole-heartedly welcomed the Bible into our lives, we have banned it. If we have relegated it to a vague guideline or a bothersome rule-book, we have banned it. We have effectively banned the Bible in our little kingdom of self.

That means it does not matter whether you live in a free country. If you are not reading the Bible – if you treat it as if it were a child occasionally allowed to chime in – then you have, in essence, rejected it. You have quietly, but effectively – for yourself – destroyed the Word.

AN ABSOLUTE YES

Our enemy cannot destroy the Word outright, but he can destroy your perspective of it. If he can turn the privilege of the Word into an obligation, if he can convince us that the Word is full of holes, if he can get us to place our own intellect above Scripture, if he can get us to let our emotions set the standards of truth, if anything other than the Word is the ultimate authority in our life – our enemy has destroyed the Word of God.

Just like at the beginning, our enemy stands next to us and asks, "Has God said … ?" Our answer to this question is key. To flat-out deny that God has said is certain destruction, for communication is cut off, and we are left to our own efforts to solve this world. But even if we say anything short of an absolute yes, we are still on a path toward destruction, just a more gradual one. For then we deceive ourselves into thinking that our own thoughts and feelings carry just as much authority as the Word of God. And our will begins to compete with God's will.

"Has God said … ?" is the question. Our response to this question will determine the direction of our lives. If we are convinced we are using something that is nearly true, this can very well result in our being nearly saved.

QUESTIONS

1. What are some misconceptions about our enemy?

2. Name some characteristics of our enemy that are vital to remember.

3. Why is it important not to underestimate or overestimate our enemy?

4. Why does our enemy consider the Word a primary target?

5. Because Satan cannot destroy the Word, what is another strategy he can use to destroy us?

6. How is religion one of Satan's best weapons?

7. How is the term "Pharisee" often misrepresented?

8. What was the main motive of the Pharisees?

9. How did the enemy undermine God's authority in Eden?

10. How has the enemy essentially banned the Bible today?

Chapter 13

THE ALMOND TREE

The issue at hand was authority. A man named Korah strongly believed that Moses and Aaron were out of line. He believed he should have just as much say in the matters at hand. Korah and about 250 others confronted the two brothers. They said, "You have gone far enough" (Numbers 16:3). Korah wanted to have some input on future decisions.

Moses set up a meeting. "Tomorrow morning the LORD will show who is His" (Numbers 16:5). It was agreed. Korah and his followers assembled the next day at the door of the tabernacle and the glory of God arrived as well. We can only assume the response was not what Korah had expected. God told Moses, "Separate yourselves from among this congregation, that I may consume them instantly" (v. 21). It was only through the intervention of Moses that any of the people survived God's anger. Korah and his group were set aside from the rest, and the earth literally opened up and swallowed them alive.

This would serve as quite a reminder about who was in charge. The Bible says Moses was the most humble man around, but authority was firmly in his hands. He and Aaron represented the authority of God. To oppose this would result in severe consequences.

Believe it or not, the very next day several others started to complain about Moses and Aaron: "You are the ones who have caused the death of the LORD's people" (Numbers 16:41). Even in the wake of Korah's extermination, these people were just not getting it. They also rose up to oppose the men God had established as authority. The response from God to Moses was the same: "Get away from among this congregation, that I may consume them instantly" (v. 45). In moments, a plague began to rip through the camp.

Moses sent Aaron on an urgent mission: "Take your censer and put in it fire from the altar, and lay incense on it; then bring it quickly to the congregation and make atonement for them, for wrath has gone forth from the LORD, the plague has begun!" (Numbers 16:46). Aaron ran.

It was only because of Aaron that everyone did not die: "He took his stand between the dead and the living, so that the plague was checked. But those who died in the plague were 14,700, besides those who died on account of Korah" (Numbers 16:48-49). If Aaron had not raced to the rescue, it would have been far worse.

At that point, God seemed to be finally getting everyone's attention, but He wanted to drive the point home. This time, the object lesson would not cost any lives: "Speak to the sons of Israel, and get from them a rod for each father's household: twelve rods, from all their leaders according to their fathers' households. You shall write each name on his rod, and write Aaron's name on the rod of Levi" (Numbers 17:2-3). The rods were then taken into the temple, into the Most Holy Place to be placed before the presence of God. When all this was set up, God made His thoughts on the matter very clear. He explained His plan to Moses: "It will come about that the rod of the man whom I choose will sprout. Thus I shall lessen from upon Myself the grumblings of the sons of Israel, who are grumbling against you" (v. 5). The question at hand was authority. God was intent on clearing up the matter.

Moses placed the 12 rods in the tabernacle and then checked on them the next day. Only Aaron's rod was different. In order to make His point, God did something miraculous: "The rod of Aaron for the house of Levi had sprouted and put forth buds and produced blossoms, and it bore ripe almonds" (Numbers 17:8). This meant something. It was not only a display of power, but a display of power that meant something.

God had Moses separate the rod of Aaron from the others. He had Moses set it aside for a specific reason: "Put back the rod of Aaron before the testimony to be kept as a sign against the rebels, that you may put an end to their grumblings against Me, so that they will not die" (Numbers 17:10). The rod came to life and produced almond blossoms in order to make a point: He wanted to make sure everyone knew where the authority was. The rebellions were to stop. Inside the ark of the covenant, a peculiar, budded rod was a reminder that Aaron and his descendants were the ones with the authority and not Korah or the ones who followed in Korah's footsteps. Authority was established, and the lesson was in the form of an almond branch.

THE LAMP

The imagery of the almond tree was nothing new. In fact, it was already in the tabernacle. When the construction of the tabernacle took place, there were meticulous instructions, including not only how it would be built but also what would be placed inside it. One of the items was a lamp.

The lamp was designed to resemble almond blossoms:

> There were six branches going out of its sides; three branches of the lampstand from the one side of it and three branches of the lampstand from the other side of it; three cups shaped like almond blossoms, a bulb and a flower in one branch, and three cups shaped like almond blossoms, a bulb and a flower in the other branch – so for the six branches going out of the lampstand. (Exodus 37:18-19)

The lampstand had seven parts, each of which was continually burning. It was the only source of light in the tabernacle. In order to see what he was doing, a priest relied on the lampstand that God designed.

This serves as a representation of the Word of God (Psalm 119:105). The Word is the Light just as Jesus is the Light (John 1:4-5). The Word reveals the world for the modern-day priest known as the Christian. It defeats darkness. It is authority. The lampstand in the tabernacle provided illumination – a precursor of the ultimate Light that would provide spiritual illumination. Nearby, on the other side of the veil in the Most Holy Place and within the ark of the covenant, was the budded rod of Aaron.

One key consideration here is that God has always been deeply involved in making sure that His authority and how it is perceived are clear. He did not leave Aaron in the midst of confusion. When the rebellions broke out against authority, God demonstrated that the issues were not up for grabs. Authority was not going to bend to the whims of Korah or anyone else who followed in his steps. [1]

A POSITION OF HUMILITY

For the modern believer, this is a strong reminder of our own position. When it comes to questioning spiritual authority, there should be some hesitation. Before anyone suggests that the Bible is less than God's perfect Word, he should consider the history of such criticisms. It is one thing to dig in and study in order to examine the integrity of the Bible, but to become part of any kind of "rebellion" against its authority is not wise. At the very least, a certain amount of humility is appropriate: "In humility receive the word implanted, which is able to save your souls" (James 1:21). Receiving the Word with anything less than humility will not serve anyone well.

When God sent out His Word, it carried His determination and power. As such, He fully expected results. In one particular analogy He described it as rain and snow:

> For as the rain and the snow come down from heaven, and do not return there without watering the earth and making it bear and sprout, and furnishing seed to the sower and bread to the eater; so will My Word be which goes forth from My mouth; it will not return to Me empty, without accomplishing what I desire, and without succeeding in the matter for which I sent it. (Isaiah 55:10-11)

When God sent out His Word, it accomplished what He desired. It did not falter in its mission.

---

1 God used Korah later as an example of those who are destructive to the church (Jude 11). The rebellion of Korah was recorded for us to learn something.

A world covered with creatures of free will can and does distort the Truth. But the Word itself was shaped and delivered with great care by the Creator. The reception is usually corrupt, but the source and the delivery are perfect.

WATCHFUL OF THE WORD

God gave Jeremiah a task very similar to our own task. Teach the truth to a world that is antagonistic to the truth. As many of us are, Jeremiah was hesitant to venture out on this mission, but God assured Jeremiah that He would be with him. Then God asked Jeremiah an interesting question. After sending Jeremiah a vision, He asked Jeremiah what he saw. This did not mean that God did not know what the vision was. Instead, you might think of it as something along the lines of "testing, testing, one, two, three." The discussion was as follows: "The Word of the LORD came to me saying, 'What do you see, Jeremiah?' And I said, 'I see a rod of an almond tree.' Then the LORD said to me, 'You have seen well, for I am watching over My word to perform it' " (Jeremiah 1:11-12). God sent an image, and the image was received correctly.

This was no random image. God did not casually sort through the vast array of His creation and just yank out the first bit of flora that caught His eye. It meant something. The lamp that was designed to look like something from an almond tree meant light, knowledge, insight and divine inspiration. And the budded rod in the recesses of the Most Holy Place meant authority, truth and finality in all moral debates. So when Jeremiah received the image of an almond tree, it was more than just a test pattern. It meant something.

It was a pun. God often used wordplay to make His point. [2] The word for almond tree also means "wakeful" because the almond tree was the first to blossom or "wake up." This word also includes the concept of

---

2 A hypothetical variation of this passage might be helpful, using a pun that works in English. Imagine that, instead of an almond branch, God sent Jeremiah an image of a well: "The Word of the LORD came to me saying, 'What do you see, Jeremiah?' And I said, 'I see a well.' Then the LORD said to me, 'You have seen well.' " Any humor we might derive from such wordplay is secondary. The primary consideration is that God is emphasizing His point.

being "watchful." This is why God said, "I am watching over My word" (Jeremiah 1:12). He was wide awake and watchful. He was involved. He was on the job. God did not just lob some truth at the earth and then hope for the best. He has always been much more involved than that.

NOTHING LESS THAN PERFECT

Consider God's nature. We know that He is fair (Deuteronomy 32:4). [3] It would be extremely unfair to allow a book to be thrown together that is reliable only most of the time. Our salvation is at stake. We know that only those who do the will of the Father will enter heaven (Matthew 7:21). It seems unlikely God would send His will clouded in a murky book of sayings. A book of partial truth would not be helpful.

As we established in the first chapter, God not only exists, but also is deeply involved in His creation. Nothing is impossible for Him, and He is all-knowing. If this is the God who truly oversees all matters, His Word is certainly going to reflect these aspects of His nature. It will be a book that was designed, produced and delivered by an Author who is all-powerful and all-knowing. Such a book would be nothing short of perfect.

God is a God of clarity. When it comes to His expectations concerning how His people will interact, we are reminded, "God is not a God of confusion" (1 Corinthians 14:33). If He expects as much from those who belong to Him, certainly He would present a book that meets the same requirements. A book that inherently contained confusion would be less than godly.

A SIMPLE CHOICE

We are faced with an extensive splintering of ideas, all heading off in a thousand different directions. But even before all of this confusion, there is a simple fork in the road. A simple choice that faces each individual. Is this the Word of God, or is it not?

If the Word is partially reliable – if it is inevitably a recipe for chaos and frustration – it is difficult to feel driven to be devoted to it. It is hard to get excited about living your life according to something that

---

3 See also Genesis 18:25; Daniel 4:37.

might be the truth. But if the Word is completely inspired, then it can serve as a source of peace and trust. Either it is not the Truth, or it is the Truth. The in-between area is where things begin to break down.

The Bible tells us that Scripture is designed so "that the man of God may be adequate, equipped for every good work" (2 Timothy 3:17). God has provided His Word. Now it comes down to whether you will accept it as such.

God is watching over His Word. It has been delivered. Now the same question God asked Jeremiah falls to you. What do you see?

QUESTIONS

1. Why did Korah and the others rebel against Moses?

2. What did the budding rod have to do with these rebellions?

3. Why was this budding rod placed inside the tabernacle?

4. Other than this rod, what other object was also patterned after the same plant? What did it represent?

5. What are some ways it is possible to be part of a "rebellion" against God's authority today?

6. Why did God show an almond tree to Jeremiah?

7. What pun is significant in relation to the word for almond tree?

8. How does the fact that God is a just God help shed light on the nature of the Word?

9. How does our perception about the Word affect our enthusiasm about developing a relationship with it?

10. What is the crucial question that God asked Jeremiah?

WORKS CONSULTED

Bauer, Walter. *A Greek Lexicon of the New Testament and Other Early Christian Literature.* Trans. and ed. William F. Arndt and F. Wilbur Gingrich. 2nd ed. Chicago: University of Chicago Press, 1979. Print.

This is a standard Greek lexicon that is an invaluable reference for biblical word studies. Definitions are bolstered by etymologies, various specific examples of usage, and root forms of relevant words.

Crist, Terry M. *Learning the Language of Babylon: Changing the World by Engaging the Culture.* Grand Rapids: Chosen Books, 2001. Print.

Using the Babylonian captivity of the people of God as a platform, this book explores significant parallels with the modern Christian's own circumstances as a "captive" in the world. One of the most insightful aspects of the book is its ability to navigate a careful balance between using the culture and being influenced by it. The author emphasizes the option of "engaging" the culture in order to reach the lost while still avoiding any compromise in our relationship with God.

Duke, Kerry. *Ox in the Ditch: Bible Interpretation As the Foundation of Christian Ethics.* **Huntsville: Publishing Designs, 1993. Print.**

> Beginning with an in-depth presentation on the infallibility of Scripture, this book approaches the concerns of today's situation ethics and various moral dilemmas. This study uses God's Old Covenant command about an ox falling into a ditch on the Sabbath to deal with "extenuating circumstances" without ignoring our covenant with God.

Fry, Paul H. *Literary Theory: Ways In and Out of the Hermeneutic Circle.* **Yale. 2010. Podcast.**

> This is a series of lectures presented at Yale. They are an extensive analysis of literary criticism, covering various styles and approaches. Although the purpose of the class is purely secular, the material addresses many of the issues that ultimately have to do with our perception of books in general and, in particular, the Scriptures.

Gaussen, Louis. *Theopneustia: The Plenary Inspiration of the Holy Scriptures.* **Charleston: Nabu, 1841. Print.**

> To a certain extent, this is a relatively obscure book. Parts of this edition are distorted due to the loss of legible original copies. It is an extended argument about biblical inspiration, emphasizing that Scripture itself should be allowed to establish the parameters of the Bible's integrity.

Geisler, Norman L. and William E. Nix. *A General Introduction to the Bible.* **Chicago: Moody, 1986. Print.**

> This serves as a thorough study about the general nature of the Bible. Addressing the inspiration, canonization, transmission and translation of the Word of God, it covers a great deal of territory regarding how the Bible was given to man. In particular, the section addressing the plenary nature of biblical inspiration offers helpful analogies.

House, H. Wayne and Gordon A. Carle. *Doctrine Twisting: How Core Biblical Truths Are Distorted.* **Downers Grove: IVP Books, 2003. Print.**

> Designed to address various doctrines and the potential threat of undermining them, this book begins by addressing this question:

"How is the Bible the Word of God?" This section assures the reader God has successfully delivered His message of salvation in an accurate and effective way.

Pink, Arthur W. *The Divine Inspiration of the Bible.* **Mulberry: Sovereign Grace Publishers, 2007. Print.**

Originally published in the 1920s, this book explores the integrity of the Bible, pinpointing specifically the unity of the text despite its numerous writers. This aspect of the Bible, along with its indestructibility in the face of drastic opposition, suggests an overall divine Author.

Smith, F. LaGard. *The Cultural Church: Winds of Change and the Call for a "New Hermeneutic."* **Nashville: 21st Century Christian, 2001. Print.**

Exploring religious trends, this book focuses on the relatively recent idea of the "new hermeneutic." The author reveals strong possibilities that this new concept results in a compromise of doctrine. He also addresses the danger of becoming a "culture-captive church."

Smith, F. LaGard. *Radical Restoration: A Call for Pure and Simple Christianity.* **Nashville: Cotswold, 2001. Print.**

This book tackles the confusion of denominationalism, objectively reexamining the status of modern congregations that claim to be the church. The concept of restoration serves as a tool for pointing out ways some congregations are successfully following the pattern of Scripture and how others might be falling short due to cultural influence.

Wells, David F. *God in the Wasteland: The Reality of Truth in a World of Fading Dreams.* **Grand Rapids: Eerdmans, 1994. Print.**

This is an extensive examination of our culture and its tendency to demean and degrade. Focusing on specific facets of our modern society, this book reveals how this post-modern world can distort our perception of what is real and what really matters.

ABOUT THE AUTHOR

Bret Carter graduated from the University of Colorado at Colorado Springs with a bachelor's degree in English. He also attended the Bear Valley Bible Institute of Denver, Colo. He lives in Westminster, Colo., where he teaches Bible, English and history at Hyland Christian School.

Along with his teaching career, he serves as editor of *Rocky Mountain Christian*, a newspaper for churches of Christ. He writes a monthly editorial for that paper and has had his writing published in secular papers as well, including *Boston Literary Magazine*. In 2005, he was a finalist in the Rocky Mountain Fiction Writers Novel Contest.

Bret attends Brighton Church of Christ, where he teaches Bible classes, preaches and leads singing.

ACKNOWLEDGMENTS

I want to thank my mom, Jean Carter, for reading through the very early drafts and for her indestructible encouragement that defines all great moms.

Lenae West was also an immense help in polishing the book.

In addition, I want to express my appreciation for those of you who took the time to read the book and give encouraging feedback: Mike Byron, Logan Cates, Marek Dawidow, Jason Looney, Matthew Morine, Scott Raab, and Dr. Denny Petrillo.

And many others who also took the time to look the material over.

Plus the ones who I have forgotten to mention here, due to my own pitiful memory. Not long from now, I will be horrified that my brain failed me at this particular moment. Rest assured – the pain of my sudden recollection of your part in all this will be in direct proportion to my heartfelt, but belated appreciation.